Landmarks of world literature

Goethe

FAUST. PART ONE

GOETHE

Faust. Part One

NICHOLAS BOYLE

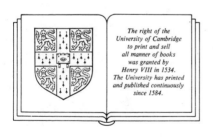

The right of the
University of Cambridge
to print and sell
all manner of books
was granted by
Henry VIII in 1534.
The University has printed
and published continuously
since 1584.

CAMBRIDGE UNIVERSITY PRESS

Cambridge
London   New York   New Rochelle
Melbourne   Sydney

Published by the Press Syndicate of the University of Cambridge
The Pitt Building, Trumpington Street, Cambridge CB2 1RP
32 East 57th Street, New York, NY 10022, USA
10 Stamford Road, Oakleigh, Melbourne 3166, Australia

First published 1987

Printed in Great Britain at
the University Press, Cambridge

British Library cataloguing in publication data

Boyle, Nicolas
Goethe: Faust. Part One. − (Landmarks
of world literature)
1. Goethe, Johann Wolfgan von, 1749–1832
I. Title   II. Series
823′.6   PT1925

Library of Congress cataloguing in publication data

Boyle, Nicholas.
Goethe, Faust. Part One.
(Landmarks of world literature)
Bibliography.
1. Goethe, Johann Wolfgang von, 1749–1832. Faust.
PT1938.B69   1986   832′.6   86–13610

ISBN 0 521 32801 2 hard covers
ISBN 0 521 31412 7 paperback

For Rosemary

Contents

Preface

The aim of this study is to give a coherent, literary, introduction to *Faust. Part One*, both for the general reader, who may have no German, and for the student who may be approaching for the first time a work which must rank among the most puzzling landmarks in modern literature. Throughout, I have taken as a maxim that the text which Goethe chose to publish can be read in such a way as to make good and rewarding sense, poetically, philosophically, and even historically. While I also hope that the more advanced student may find here some new ideas, the nature of the series to which this volume belongs precludes any underpinning – or decorating – of the structure with the traditional scholarly apparatus. The principal argument for any particular interpretation which might appear controversial is always the general coherence of the account to which it contributes.

The German text of *Faust*, and line references to it, are given in accordance with volume 3 of the Hamburger Ausgabe of Goethe's works, edited by Erich Trunz (Hamburg, 1949). These references (given as simple numbers, italicised to distinguish them from dates) will also serve as references to the line-by-line translation in the Norton Critical Edition (*Johann Wolfgang von Goethe, Faust. A Tragedy. Backgrounds and Sources. The Author on the Drama. Contemporary Reactions. Modern Criticism,* translated by Walter Arndt, edited by Cyrus Hamlin, New York, 1976). Page references are given to two other readily available translations: the Penguin Edition (*Faust. Part One*, translated by Philip Wayne, Harmondsworth, 1984; first published 1949), and the Everyman Edition (*Goethe's Faust. Parts I and II,* translated by Sir Theodore Martin. Revised, with introduction and notes, by W. H. Bruford, London, 1971; first issued 1954 [Martin's translation of *Part One* first appeared in 1865]). For the sake of literal accuracy, however, all the translations given here are my own.

I should like to express my gratitude to the Alexander von Humboldt Foundation, whose support enabled me to undertake much of the preliminary work for this study. I am grateful too to my colleagues, particularly Dr J. Cameron Wilson, for so generously taking over my other responsibilities while I have been writing it. Professor J. P. Stern made many valuable suggestions. To my wife, however, this book, and therefore its reader, owes most, and to her it is dedicated.

N.B.

Chronology

	Goethe's life and works	Historical and cultural events
1740		Maria Theresa Empress in Austria; Frederick II (the Great) King in Prussia; Fielding: *Tom Jones*
1749	28 August: Goethe born in Frankfurt on the Main	
1756–63		Seven Years War
1759		Lessing: *Faust* scene
1765–8	Studies in Leipzig	
1770–1	Studies in Strasbourg; meets Herder; love affair with Friederike Brion; poems	
1771	Shakespearean historical drama, *Götz von Berlichingen*; 'Storm and Stress' period begins	Herder edits *Of German Character and Art* – 'Storm and Stress' manifesto
1773	First work on *Faust*; many small dramas, including *Satyros*	
1774	Novel in letters, *The Sorrows of Young Werther*, a European best seller	
1775	Engagement to Lili Schönemann broken off; invited to Weimar by Duke Karl August (aged 18); work on *Faust* interrupted	P. Weidmann: *Johann Faust*; J. M. R. Lenz: *Pandaemonium Germanikum*; Sheridan: *The Rivals*

Year	Goethe	Historical and cultural events
1776	(to 1786) growing administrative and theatrical responsibilities in Weimar; friendship with Charlotte von Stein; 'Principal insight that ultimately all things are ethical'	American Declaration of Independence; 'Painter' Müller: *Faust's Life Dramatised* (and 1778)
1781	Ennobled, becoming 'von Goethe'	Kant: *Critique of Pure Reason*; Schiller: *The Robbers*; G. C. Tobler: essay on *Nature*
1782	Rewrites *Werther*; obtains extended leave from Weimar and departs secretly for Italy; completes classicising drama *Iphigenia in Tauris*	J. H. Füssli (Fuseli): *The Nightmare*
1786		Frederick the Great dies; Mozart: *The Marriage of Figaro*; Tischbein: *Goethe in the Campagna*
1787	Visits Naples, Sicily, Rome; completes drama, *Egmont*; work on *Faust* (*Witch's Kitchen, Forest, Cavern*)	Blake: *Songs of Innocence*
1788	Returns to Weimar as poet, rather than administrator; begins living with Christiane Vulpius	Botany Bay settled; Schiller: *The Gods of Greece*
1789	Completes *Tasso*, tragedy of a poet; first, and only surviving, child (August) born	14 July, Bastille stormed in Paris ('the Revolution'); Lavoisier: *Elementary Treatise on Chemistry*
1790	*Faust. A Fragment* published; turns to optics and botany; reads Kant	Emperor Joseph II dies; Flaxman: Illustrations to Homer
1791	Director of Weimar Court Theatre	F. M. Klinger: *Faust's Life . . .*, novel
1792	On Allied campaign in France; at Valmy	Danton; Allies retreat from Valmy; French Republic begins

1793		David, *Death of Marat*
1794	Friendship with Schiller begins	Fall of Robespierre
1795	Novel, *Wilhelm Meister's Years of Apprenticeship*, published (also 1796)	Schiller: *Aesthetic Letters*
1796	Classical poems: *Alexis and Dora, Hermann and Dorothea*	Bonaparte's Italian campaign
1797	Resumes work on *Faust* (*Dedication, Prelude, Prologue*)	Hölderlin: *Hyperion*; Schlegel's Shakespeare translation begins; Wackenroder: *Lucubrations of a Monastic Art-Lover*
1798	*Prison* scene versified; starts classicising journal, *The Propylaea*	Bonaparte in Egypt; Schelling appointed professor in Jena; Schiller: *Wallenstein*; Wordsworth: *Lyrical Ballads*; Schlegels start Romantic journal, *Athenaeum*
1799	Starts neo-classical Weimar art competition; work on *Faust*	Schleiermacher: *On Religion*; Novalis: *Christendom, or Europe*; Fichte leaves Jena (atheism controversy)
1800	Much work on *Faust*, including Helena scenes for Part Two	Fichte: *On the Vocation of Man*
1801	Serious illness; work on *Faust* interrupted; work on *Theory of Colours* (to 1810)	
1803	Finishes *The Natural Daughter*, play about French Revolution	Territorial reorganisation of Holy Roman Empire by Napoleon; Beethoven: *Third Symphony* (Eroica)

1804	.	Napoleon crowned emperor; Chamisso: *Faust*
1805	Ends art competition	Trafalgar; Hegel appointed professor in Jena
1806	Work on *Walpurgis Night*; 13 April, *Faust. Part One* finished; Goethe's house spared during looting of Weimar after battle of Jena; marries Christiane Vulpius	Holy Roman Empire ends; Battle of Jena: Prussia defeated
1807	Starts novel, *Wilhelm Meister's Years of Wandering*	Hegel: *Phenomenology of Mind*
1808	*Faust. Part One* published; meets Napoleon	Peninsular Campaign begins; Kleist: *Penthesilea*
1809	*The Elective Affinities*, novel	
1810	*Theory of Colours* published; *Pandora*, drama	Regency begins in England; Mme de Staël: *On Germany*; C. D. Friedrich: *Monk beside the Sea*; Goya: *Disasters of War*
1811	First part of autobiography, *Poetry and Truth*, published (completed 1831)	P. Cornelius: *Faust-Cycle*; Schubert: Goethe settings (to 1826)
1813		Napoleon defeated at Leipzig
1814	Poems in Persian style of Hafiz begin; interest in medieval art revives	Scott: *Waverley*; Jane Austen: *Mansfield Park*; Chamisso: *Peter Schlemihl*
1815		Waterloo; Congress of Vienna concluded

1816	Partial production of *Faust* in Berlin; wife, Christiane, dies: 'emptiness and deathly silence in and around me'; *Italian Journey*, Part One (completed 1829); schema for *Faust. Part Two* (unpublished)	Coleridge: *Kubla Khan*; Constant: *Adolphe*; F. A. M. Retzsch: illustrations to *Faust*
1818	Reads translation of Marlowe's *Doctor Faustus*	Keats: *Endymion*; Mrs Shelley: *Frankenstein*; Grillparzer: *Sappho*
1819	*West-Eastern Divan*, Persian-style poems	Carlsbad Decrees; Schopenhauer: *The World as Will and Idea*
1820		George IV King of England; first partial English versions of *Faust*; Shelley: *Prometheus Unbound*
1821	*Wilhelm Meister's Years of Wandering*, first edition (second, 1829)	Greek War of Independence begins; Byron dedicates *Sardanapalus* to Goethe; Constable: *The Hay Wain*
1823	First conversation with J. P. Eckermann; *Marienbad Elegy*	Gower: Translation of *Faust*; Beethoven: *Ninth Symphony*
1825	Resumes work on *Faust*	Decembrist revolt in Russia; Stockton to Darlington railway
1827	*Helena, a classical-romantic phantasmagoria. Interlude for 'Faust'* (i.e. Act Three of *Part Two*) published; reads Manzoni's *The Betrothed*; correspondence with Carlyle	Heine: *Book of Songs*; Hugo: *Preface to 'Cromwell'*; Delacroix: illustrations to Stapfer's French translation of *Faust*
1828	Part of Act One of *Faust. Part Two* published	

1829	Numerous productions of *Faust. Part One* to celebrate Goethe's eightieth birthday, but he attends none of them	Balzac: *Les Chouans*; Turner: *Ulysses Deriding Polyphemus*
1830	Finishes Acts One and Two of *Faust. Part Two*; son dies	July Revolution in France; Hugo: *Hernani*; Stendhal: *Scarlet and Black*
1831	Act Five, then Act Four of *Part Two*, completed 22 July	Hegel dies
1832	Dies 22 March	Second Reform Bill in England; Scott, Bentham die
1833	*Faust. Part Two* published	

Chapter 1

Goethe and the Faust tradition

Johann Wolfgang Goethe is the supreme genius of modern German literature and has been the dominant influence in German literary culture since the middle of the eighteenth century. His poems, dramas, novels, essays, scientific writings and letters run in published form to 138 volumes, not including nine volumes of drawings and watercolours and four large volumes of official correspondence. He provided Europe, from the Romantic Movement to the early twentieth century, with her conception of poetry and the poet's role, and he fathered a dynasty of nineteenth-century and post-nineteenth-century sages, from Thomas Carlyle to Matthew Arnold, Benedetto Croce and Ortega y Gasset. His *Faust* is certainly the greatest long poem of modern European literature. Throughout his life of eighty-two years he showed himself responsive to every new cultural movement not only in Germany but in Western Europe in general, though his first loyalty was to a rather specialised classicism of his own defini-tion. He also retained a benign if remote interest in the affairs of North America. For sixty years of a lifetime during which the world changed radically he was occupied, at intervals, with the writing of *Faust*: a first version was written shortly before the American Declaration of Independence; its first, fragmentary, publication fell in the year after the storming of the Bastille; *Faust. Part One* was published in the heyday of the Napoleonic Empire, between the battle of Jena and the retreat from Moscow; and *Faust. Part Two* was completed in the aftermath of the revolution in France of July 1830, to which some of its last scenes make allusion. But behind this long process there lay already three centuries of tradition.

I   From Faust-Book to *Urfaust*

The myth of Faust is one of the few authentic myths of the modern era, comparable in its popular and artistic appeal only to the myth of Don Juan, with which it has subterranean connections. But there actually was a Doctor Faust. For the anthropologist and psychoanalyst the story of the magician who sells his soul to the Devil may have roots going far deeper into the past than the sixteenth century. But for the literary historian the career of Dr Faust begins around 1480, with the birth of Georg Faust in the small town of Knittlingen in Württemberg, south-west Germany. Of the studies which may have justified his academic title nothing is known, though he seems to have been associated with Heidelberg and later with Wittenberg and was a personal acquaintance of the great Reformer Philipp Melanchthon, who however knew him under the name of John (Johann(es)). An astrologer and high-class mountebank, Faust had enough confidence and success to be employed to cast the horoscopes of the rich and powerful, though he was forced into a wandering life by debts, pederasty and charges of witchcraft − the last probably encouraged by Faust himself. Stories of a pact with the Devil, a flight through the air, magical military assistance to the Emperor and the summoning up of the spirits of Homeric antiquity circulated during his lifetime, perhaps products of his own publicity machine. After his death, possibly from unnatural causes, in 1540 or 1541, these stories and others, probably older than he, gathered around his memory and were collected in manuscript, both in Latin and in German. Such a collection was first printed in Frankfurt in 1587. The compiler was anonymous, the publisher was Johann Spiess, and the title, *The History of Dr John Faust. The Far-Famed Magician and Nigromancer*, confirmed the renaming of the man who during his life had preferred to call himself Georgius Sabellicus, the Sabine area of Italy being famous for its witches. At this point the story of Faust enters into literature.

Spiess's publication, known in modern German as a

Volksbuch − meaning, roughly, 'chap-book' − is little more than a sequence of separately titled incidents. After a brief account, already remote from historical fact, of Faust's parentage and his brilliant university career, we are told how he conjured up the Devil, first in the terrifying shape of a fiery man and then in the form of a grey friar. There follow three conversations with this more approachable spirit, Mephostophiles by name, before Faust signs in blood the agreement by which he surrenders himself body and soul to Hell once twenty-four years have elapsed, during which time Mephostophiles is bound to fulfil his every wish. The service the Devil offers, to which the greater part of the book is devoted, is dull stuff, however: answers to esoteric queries, such as why winter and summer are reversed in the southern hemisphere; rapid transport to far-off and for Spiess's readership exciting places, such as the seraglio in Constantinople, or the architectural wonders of Florence; magical tricks performed on a gaping populace − Faust eats a wagonload of straw and strikes dumb a herd of vexatiously lowing cattle; or the summoning up of figures from the past, particularly Helen of Troy, who becomes his concubine and with whom he begets a son. A semblance of narrative tension is maintained by Faust's frequent accesses of remorse, but he is prevented from revoking the pact by Mephostophiles' threat that to do so will bring his life to an immediate and bloody end. But that end awaits Faust anyway, and when the twenty-four years have passed, concluding with a night of fearful expectation and vain attempts at repentance, the Devil fetches Faust as agreed, and the story reaches a grisly, no doubt edifying, but hardly unexpected conclusion. That indeed, for the solidly orthodox, Lutheran, narrator, is the point: Faust's life, though full of entertaining, if uncanny, marvels, seems to him a protracted and perverse disregard of the obvious. The only explanation he can give of Faust's turning from theology to magic is that 'it was Dr Faust's intent to love that which ought not to be loved . . . he took to himself eagle's wings, and wished to seek out the grounds of all things in heaven and on earth'. But because, in the narrator's eyes, this ambition is not in any circumstances proper to man, it cannot be fulfilled even by magical means. Throughout, the narrator is at pains to remind his readership that Mephostophiles is permanently deceiving Faust – the knowledge, visions and pleasures that Faust acquires are all false, and Faust has bartered his soul for nothing, for a vain pretence.

From the 1587 Faust-Book there emerged two lines of tradition which eventually percolated into the literary consciousness of the later eighteenth century. The first might be called the chap-book line. *The History of Dr John Faust* was only the first of a series of collections which grew larger as more incidents and more moralising footnotes were added: that of Widmann (1599) already ran to over 600 pages, and that of Pfitzer (1674), which Goethe is known to have consulted in 1801, and possibly earlier, was not much shorter. The *Book of Faust, by One of a Christian Persuasion* (1725) is by comparison a brief digest and its various editions were, in the eighteenth century, the most common printed form of the Faust legend. The larger compilations were much rarer and the book *By One of a Christian Persuasion* is the only Faust-Book the young Goethe is at all likely to have seen. Throughout his life Goethe seems to have remained unaware of Spiess's publication, the first origin of his own masterpiece.

What is certain, from Goethe's own avowal, is that he knew something of the second line of descent, the dramatic line. The first Faust-Book of 1587 was translated into English not later than 1592, and at some time between 1588 and 1593 the genius of Christopher Marlowe impressed on this robustly didactic but shapeless material a dramatic form so persuasive and so haunting that it has left its mark on practically all subsequent retellings of Faust's story, Goethe's not excluded.

In Marlowe's *Tragicall History of the Life and Death of Doctor Faustus* the proportions of Spiess's publication are drastically altered in the interests of theatrical effect, so that the weight of attention lies on the beginning and the end of Faustus' career, the two peaks of emotion in his life: his turning from God to the Devil, and the last hours of waiting for damnation. The single greatest stroke of Marlowe's genius is the invention of the opening monologue, in which Faustus rejects the traditional branches of learning in favour of magic, the nigromantic art. This opening monologue is characteristic of almost every subsequent dramatic treatment of the Faust story, but was unnecessary in the original Faust-Book, whose omniscient narrator could articulate Faust's thoughts and motives, and perhaps felt obliged in religion to do so, without calling on Faust to articulate them himself. Left to himself, Faust might have been too convincing. Other long-lived motifs incorporated or invented by Marlowe are: Faustus' use of a 'damned booke' to gain access to the spirit world; a conjuring scene, over which Lucifer himself presides, and in which the Devil appears, first in a terrifyingly destructive form, then in the shape of a friar and under the name of Mephostopholis; two distinct conversations with Mephostopholis, in between which Mephostopholis gets permission from his master Lucifer to conclude a pact with Faustus; the pact itself, sealed in Faustus' blood to the accompaniment of ominous signs and despite pleadings from the angels of Heaven not to turn away from God; a sequence of incidents of a more or less farcical kind and involving a clown who attempts to reproduce Faustus' magical feats – these include the visit to the Imperial German Court and the summoning of Helen; and a final monologue in which an agonised Faustus watches his last hours elapse before the Devil comes to take his due. The tension which is occasionally renewed in the long, flat central section of the chap-book by Faust's sudden pangs of remorse is provided in Marlowe's play by a conflict between Good and Bad Angels who dispute the possession of Faustus' conscience. That these disputes regularly issue in Faustus' reiteration of his determination to be damned indicates a profounder transformation by Marlowe of his source. The only motive the chap-book could find for Faust's diabolism was a perverse desire for forbidden or inaccessible knowledge. Marlowe's Faustus, by contrast, is impelled by a desire for personal power and fulfilment, which is presented – perhaps – as excessive, but certainly not as eccentric or inhuman. It is the constraints on that desire which appear as unnatural, as unobvious:

> O what a world of profite and delight,
> Of power, of honour, of omnipotence,
> Is promised to the Studious Artizan? . . .
> A sound Magitian is a Demi-god.

This is the ambition, not of an over-curious scholar, but of Marlowe's world-devouring Tamburlaine. There is therefore no equivalent in Marlowe's play to the chap-book's emphasis on the vanity and deceitfulness of the Devil's gifts; nor does the association of a clown with Faustus' enterprises cast an ironic or comical light on the principal figure himself. None the less Marlowe's tragedy, though it continued to be performed until the Restoration period, had no significant posterity in England, and the theme was increasingly confined to pantomime and burlesque, in which form the story made occasional stage appearances until well into the eighteenth century.

Throughout the first half of the seventeenth century troupes of English players, clowns and acrobats toured the German Empire performing, in a mixture of English and German, plays which included debased versions of works by Shakespeare and Marlowe. A performance of *Doctor Faustus* in Graz is recorded as early as 1608. From these English performances there derived, in all probability, the popular versions of the Faust story, in the German language, which continued to be played by travelling actors throughout Germany for over a century after the last English troupes had left. Performances are known, for example, to have taken place in Frankfurt in 1767 and in Hamburg in 1770. Faust thus returned to his native country, where he was so thoroughly renaturalised that to Voltaire in 1767 'votre fameux docteur Faustus' seemed exclusively German property. Voltaire was plainly happy for him to remain so. As far as one can judge, these German stage versions retained Marlowe's dramatic outline, though much effaced by special effects, pyrotechnics and, from the late seventeenth century onwards, the influence of Italian comedy.

From these already dramatic versions of the Faust story, rather than from the chap-books, we should derive the Faust puppet-plays of the seventeenth and eighteenth centuries, which are the only form of the legend whose direct influence Goethe publicly acknowledged. Even though the marionettes might be large – three feet high – and the effects ingenious, with perhaps two or three puppet-masters, a puppet-theatre was much more economical and mobile than a troupe of actors, who would anyway always prefer a contract with a princely court theatre to the wandering life, and so these miniature semi-mechanical theatres provided much of the popular entertainment throughout the German provinces until the early nineteenth century. Just as the trade was dying out, literary scholars collected the often closely guarded scripts by which the puppet-masters made their living, and this material gives us some idea of the plot of a late-eighteenth-century *Faust* puppet-play. There might be a prologue in Hell, in which Satan would resolve to tempt Faust, perhaps because of his outstanding intellect; there would certainly be a monologue by Faust during which, with the aid of a book, he would conjure up several devils, of whom one, Mephistopheles, after various transformations, would subside into human shape and become Faust's familiar. After the usual two conversations, a pact would be made, for example for the duration of twenty-four years of 365 days each, and the incidents would begin. During these, and perhaps already in the introductory material, a prominent role would be given to the clown, Kasperle or Hans Wurst. In some versions the clown even provides a sardonic commentary on the last three hours of Faust's life – at regular intervals the clock strikes, a voice off-stage announces successively 'Fauste, accusatus es', 'Fauste, judicatus es', 'Fauste, in aeternum damnatus es' ('Faust you are accused, judged, condemned for all eternity'), Faust laments his lot, and the clown, now a nightwatchman – a secure job he has obtained by a judicious use of Faust's devils which has not involved him in any dangerous pact – calls the hour himself, adding some jeering or comical verses. In such a puppet-play Faust appears as partly a figure of fun:

for all his knowledge and art he is not half so clever as the cunning and worldly wise Hans Wurst. He may even find his end sprung upon him unexpectedly after only twelve years, when Mephistopheles reveals to him that in making the pact he counted only the days and forgot to include the 365 nights which every year also contains.

The course by which Marlowe's play had declined, to become the German equivalent of Punch and Judy, was not known in the eighteenth century. Goethe himself probably did not read Marlowe's *Faustus* until 1818, and he seems not to have realised its historical significance. Around 1750, German literary intellectuals began to look into their national past for themes and forms of a native dramatic tradition that could be revived to counter the influence of French classical models, and to stand one day beside the non-classical achievement of Shakespeare. Ironically, perhaps, they early turned in this search to the debased reincarnation of one of the greatest works of Shakespeare's principal rival. G. E. Lessing – critic, dramatist and latterly theologian: in a sense, the German Voltaire – showed more critical intuition than he ever realised when he wrote, in the seventeenth of his *Literary Letters* (1759), during his campaign against the French connection, 'that our old plays really were very much in the English style', and that the German 'Doctor Faust' 'has many scenes which only a Shakespearean genius can have been capable of conceiving'.

Lessing's own attempt to write a native German tragedy on the Faust theme has not survived, if it was ever completed. But the fragments published by his literary executors in 1784 suggest a fundamental incompatibility between Lessing's modern religious convictions and the traditional form of the legend in which, as a patriotic literary innovator, he wished to embody them. Between the simple Lutheranism which had first told the story of Faust and the sophisticated Enlightenment which sought to revive it there had intervened a great shift in the religious foundations of German culture (a shift which was somewhat later to be felt more widely in European culture as a whole). The theological certainties which had made Faust's crime awesome and his end inevitable were fading – Lessing indeed made it a principal part of his life's work to attack them. In the eighteenth century a tragedy of any kind was difficult to write – a tragedy on so theological a subject as Faust was next to inconceivable.

Unlike Marlowe's Faustus, Lessing's Faust, it would appear, was not to have been ensnared by 'the vaine pleasure of foure and twenty yeares' but by his only and dominating passion, by his *Wissbegierde*. This 'lust for knowledge' Lessing, not unnaturally, since his life was devoted to the spreading of the Enlightenment, regarded as the supreme human characteristic, and – not unnaturally, therefore – he was unwilling to let his Faust come to the traditional end. Faust was, at the end of the play, to seem on the point of being carried off by devils, but thereupon an angel was to appear announcing that after all Faust's desire for knowledge was not criminal, was indeed created and confirmed by God Himself: 'the Godhead did not give man the noblest of instincts in order to make him wretched'. The whole play so far was to have been no more than a dream, during which Faust was asleep. Faust was to awake and thank the higher powers for their timely warning against intellectual arrogance. Lessing's *Faust* fragments have considerable historical importance, for they inaugurate the modern tradition of non-tragic Fausts, of Fausts who are noble and representative of humanity, rather than criminal outsiders, however grandiose. The literary importance of these fragments, like that of most other eighteenth-century Fausts, is minimal.

It is not however to Lessing but to a much more obscure figure that the honour attaches of being the first writer to send Dr Faust to Heaven. Paul Weidmann's *Johann Faust*, first performed in Prague in 1775, is a prose drama in which the unities of time and place are largely observed, the events all occurring in Faust's luxurious palace and being confined to his last day on earth. Faust is presented, in a spirit of rationalist realism, as a worldling who has lived for the last twenty years a life of every conceivable vice, recently with his mistress, who happens to be called Helena.

A mysterious agreement made with a friend by the name of Mephistopheles has nearly reached its term, and Faust is consumed by melancholy. Faust's two companions, Ithuriel and Mephistopheles, appear no different from the other characters when in their company, but when alone together they reveal themselves as the good and bad angels of Marlowe and the puppet-plays, conversing uninhibitedly about life in the heavenly courts. Faust as a character is not unlike Mellefont, the hero-villain of Lessing's *Miss Sara Sampson* (1755): he is a typical figure of the sentimental Enlightenment, a sinner whose heart is not yet wholly corrupted, more weak than wicked. Despite various culminating atrocities, Faust in the last minutes of his life expresses repentance, praying to God: 'Preserve me, lest your enemies be able to say: behold, he has made beings in order to torment them.' Unlike Marlowe's Faustus, who prays in vain for a drop of Christ's blood streaming in the firmament, Weidmann's Faust is not too late. In a pantomime transformation scene Mephistopheles and the Furies are cast into darkness and a transfigured Ithuriel leads the repentant sinner off to the heavenly throne. The reason for the salvation of Weidmann's Faust is not really theological, however – the entire play preserves an embarrassed silence about theological aspects of the plot, such as the pact, except in the conversations between Mephistopheles and Ithuriel. Weidmann's Faust is saved in accordance with the Sentimental doctrine that there is no evil that a strong dose of penitent feeling and sympathetic understanding cannot undo. That doctrine renders untragic many an eighteenth-century play – such as *Miss Sara Sampson* – in which no theological issues are raised at all.

The intellectual loyalties of J. F. Müller, an acquaintance of Goethe's known as Müller the Painter, were, at any rate initially, very different from those of Lessing and Weidmann. Yet the fragments of his *Faust's Life Dramatised* published in 1776 and 1778 testify to the same difficulty in envisaging Faust as a truly tragic, as a self-destructive, character. Indeed, for each of these writers Faust embodies a human characteristic so universal and so important that he is, rather, self-justifying. For Lessing that characteristic is the thirst for knowledge. For Weidmann it is the capacity for repentant feeling, the good heart. For Müller it is the ruthless desire to transcend circumstance. Faust, for him, is an embodiment of the 'Storm and Stress' generation, to which Müller himself belonged. During the 1770s this group of angry young men, Goethe himself prominent among them, briefly transformed the face of German literature. They made themselves notorious by their cult of freedom, in matters both of literary form and of social and moral behaviour, and by their confidence in the powers and privileges of their own exceptional genius. In the Preface to his fragment of 1778 Müller wrote:

When I was a child Faust was always one of my favourite heroes, for I immediately saw in him a great fellow; a fellow who . . . had courage enough to cast down whatever crossed his path and tried to hinder him . . . small wonder if the strong man, the great fellow takes his due . . . in despite of justice and laws.

In 1820 Müller confessed in a letter that, in trying to complete his story of a genius Faust, pestered by small-town philistines, he had been unable to decide whether to consign Faust finally to Hell, as the legend required, or to Heaven where his instinct told him this notable figure belonged. Müller was no more able than Lessing or Weidmann to envisage the ultimate frustration of what he regarded as human goodness − to form, that is, a conception of tragedy. Moreover, neither Lessing nor Weidmann nor Müller was capable of seeing Faust comically either. Their Fausts are not tragically divided, as is Marlowe's, but neither are they the learned crank of the puppet-plays, or the Devil's gull of the chapbook. Their Fausts are figures to be taken with solemn seriousness, for they embody a value − intellectual curiosity, a melting heart, sheer self-assertion − which the writer takes with solemn seriousness. It was for Goethe, in the first unpublished version of his *Faust*, generally known as *Urfaust*, to recapture the older, more quizzical view of the traditional hero and at the same time to recover his original tragic aura.

II   *Urfaust*

Goethe's *Urfaust* is distinct from the *Fausts* of the Enlightenment, to which Lessing, Weidmann and Müller all variously belong, in two respects: it is a genuine Faust story, and it is a genuine tragedy. While regaining the theme for high literature, and for the most serious reflection about the human condition, Goethe has retained the national and popular character of his principal source, the puppet-play.

Urfaust is the name given, by the late-nineteenth-century scholars who discovered it, to a manuscript, not in Goethe's hand, which preserves the state to which his work on *Faust* had advanced after a period of hectic creativity falling principally in the years 1773 to 1775. With one small exception all the scenes it contains recur in *Faust. Part One*, though some are there versified or otherwise reworked (see the scenes marked with an asterisk in the table on pp. 23–4). It is not so much a separate play as a stage in the composition of *Faust. Part One*, of which indeed it is the dramatic kernel. None the less this 'almost finished' play, as a contemporary called it on hearing it read, has an integrity, and almost a unity, of its own: thirty pages of intense poetry or poetic prose – twenty vividly pictorial, detached episodes that tell their moving story with the artless allusiveness of a Border ballad. Because fifteen of these scenes are devoted to Faust's disastrous love for Margarete, or Gretchen, a simple girl from a small provincial town, and because this love story has only the slightest warrant in the traditional Faust legend, some critics have doubted whether the *Urfaust* should be regarded as a Faust play at all.

The love of Faust and Gretchen, the birth of a child whom Gretchen kills, for fear of the social consequences, her condemnation for infanticide, the violent deaths of other members of her family, her delirium and final refusal of rescue at the hands of a Faust aided by the evil Mephistopheles, all constitute a drama which might seem more characteristic of an age which knew Richardson's *Clarissa* and was rocked by Storm and Stress, than of the sixteenth-century setting of the original Faust-Book. But the early and middle eighteenth century was a time when the subject matter of modern literature — the reflection of contemporary social and subjective life in freedom from traditional myths and stories — was only uncertainly established. It is characteristic of that age to give literary status to the new subject matter by inserting it into some still traditional narrative pattern. The title-pages of the time abound in New Eloisas, New Amadises, New Menozas, New Melusinas, even New Robinsons. No one would look askance at the Gretchen episodes if Goethe's play were called *Der neue Faust*, on the analogy of Rousseau's *La nouvelle Héloïse*. Moreover, these episodes are inseparable from the pattern in which they are placed, and the pattern is unmistakably that of a Faust play.

Most notably, the *Urfaust* has the hall-mark of all Faust dramas derivative from Marlowe: the opening monologue. The magic book, too, has the prominent position given it in the puppet-plays, and with its aid Goethe's Faust, like his forebears, conjures up first a spirit 'in terrible shape', known here as the Spirit of Earth, a name which in some cabbalistic works signifies the Devil. In the later scene, *Dark Day, Countryside*, Faust says that Mephistopheles was sent to him by the Spirit of Earth, as in some puppet-plays Mephistopheles is shown to be sent by Satan. There is in the *Urfaust* no pact scene, though an agreement between Faust and Mephistopheles is briefly referred to later (1.490, *Part One 2638*). The significance of this omission should not be overemphasised, however. In the puppet-plays the pact-scene has less weight than the conjuration scene, since it is less spectacular, and even in the chap-book and Marlowe the two episodes are of nearly equal importance.

The structure of what follows remains that of a Faust story, even though the proportions are different. There is a series of incidents, at first semi-farcical: an interview between Mephistopheles and a student, a scene in which Faust entertains the carousers in Auerbach's Cellar in Leipzig, and then the Gretchen story, which begins in the same lusty and brutal tone as the scene in Auerbach's Cellar. The play ends with a period of misery and remorse, first for Gretchen, then for Faust, as time runs out and a fatal hour – the hour of Gretchen's execution – approaches. At the last, rejected by Gretchen, who bids him farewell 'for ever', Faust disappears with Mephistopheles, just as the hero of the puppet-play was whisked off the stage to Hell. The only obvious omissions, apart from the pact, are that there is no scene at the Imperial Court, nor – unless Gretchen is her 'new' counterpart – is there a Helen.

Furthermore, Goethe's 'new' Faust, with its concentration on the Gretchen episode, is in a sense an improvement on the traditional play. It is a weakness of Marlowe's drama, as of the plays deriving from it, that the emotional high points lie at the beginning and end of Faust's career, while the middle is relatively flat and directionless. Goethe creates a third high point in the centre, with the kiss that seals the love of Faust and Gretchen. When he came to think a Second Part of *Faust* necessary, Goethe constructed a fourth high point, in a similar moment of union between Faust and Helen. But what causes the peculiarly crushing effect of the conclusion to the *Urfaust* is its being the only one of Goethe's versions of *Faust* in which the denouement of the Gretchen story coincides unambiguously with the traditional denouement of the Faust story. The scene *Prison*, in which all Faust's great gifts and ambitions end in dereliction, derangement and death, evokes a true sense of tragic waste, without parallel in eighteenth-century poetry, except perhaps in *The Rime of the Ancient Mariner*. Certainly we find nothing like it in the Faust dramas of the Enlightenment, whose treatment of the traditional material is far more cavalier than Goethe's.

The heroes of Enlightenment *Fausts* all receive in the end a seal of solemn approval from their authors. In this they differ both from the comic or even foolish Fausts of the puppet-play and chap-book, and also from Marlowe's tragic hero. The inclusion of the Gretchen story in *Urfaust*, as in *Faust. Part One*, creates, however, a critical distance between the audience and the principal character. Paradoxically, it is this distance which makes it possible for Goethe's play to be a tragedy as no other version of the story had been since Marlowe's — albeit an ironical and moral tragedy, rather than the original theological tragedy, of which the possibility had long since disappeared. Goethe has written a play in which Faust is seen to be justly damned, not because he has made an agreement with the Devil, but because of what he has done to Gretchen. And that he has done because he is Faust, the man who appears in that scene most indispensable to the entire tradition of Faust plays: the opening monologue, in which Faust casts aside traditional restraints in favour of a life beyond good and evil. The Gretchen story is intrinsically connected to the Faust story because it is the story of the tragic conclusion to Faust's overweening ambition. Müller was unconcerned at the destructiveness of a 'great fellow' who was prepared to tread down anything standing in his way: Goethe saw in that claim of would-be genius to be dispensed from moral restrictions the potential for tragic guilt. Perhaps in his own life he felt the temptation to make that claim — certainly he could see the claim being made in the lives and works of the Storm and Stress generation around him. Müller eventually went to Rome to pursue his painting career, leaving behind the woman he had used and discarded, who died in penury. In 1771 Goethe himself had brutally terminated his first adult love affair, with Friederike Brion: immediately afterwards he was to see how cruel could be the end of a woman left to face alone the social consequences of an unacceptable liaison. His remorseful imagination was at its most receptive at the time of the trial and execution in 1772 of the Frankfurt infanticide, Susanna Margarete Brandt, of which every detail must have been known to him. *Urfaust* owes its unique complexity to its fusing, from the start, the public passions of a contemporary intellectual and cultural movement with a personal — emotional and moral — crisis. Goethe and Müller may have agreed in interpreting Faust as a Storm and Stress figure. The difference is that Goethe also wrote the story of Gretchen, of a *victim* of the Faustian Storm and Stress, and so made his drama from its very inception a drama of love.

III   From *Urfaust* to *Faust. Part One*

After arriving in Weimar at the end of 1775 Goethe turned gradually into a busy man of affairs who seemed and perhaps wished to put his turbulent literary youth behind him. During his stay in Italy in 1786–8 he resumed work on *Faust*, but his new scheme for the play was too ambitious to be completed in time for the first collected edition of his works, which he wanted to finish before he was forty. In 1790, under the title *Faust. A Fragment*, he published, effectively, the *Urfaust*, with three new scenes added, but without the tragic denouement, and turned his attention to natural science and to promoting classical art and literature. From 1797 onwards, at the urging of Schiller, once the last of the Storm and Stress dramatists and now his close friend, he worked frequently at the play which by 1800 he had decided to divide into two parts. In April 1801 however he seems to have lost the taste for these 'barbarities', as he called them, with their Germanic subject-matter and irregular form, and turned once more to the classical culture of Greece and Rome. None the less, when in 1806 he was again under pressure to furnish copy for another collected edition, he found that only two months' work sufficed for the editorial decisions that now gave his work a final, or rather a provisionally final, form. For even now he handed over his manuscript to his publisher under the title 'First Part of the Tragedy', with preliminary material that looked forward to further parts to come, and in the private knowledge that he could perfectly well have extended, or even added to, the existing scenes. Why this slow progress, and why this reluctance to put to the work the last full stop?

A superficial reason, at least in the early years, might have been the difficulty of conceiving the missing pact scene: of finding a way in which a modern Faust might bind himself to the Devil, a way that was plausible and poetically coherent with what was already written. Although the outlines of a solution had probably been reached by 1790 (see the note on lines *1712–1867* in Chapter 3), a new and greater problem had taken its place. The new conception of the play underlying

Faust. A Fragment seems to have been that Faust, by his agreement with the Devil, should embark on a retracing of the whole gamut of human experience which it would be the business of the play to depict. In this encyclopaedic scheme the relationship with Gretchen, instead of being, as in the *Urfaust*, the dramatically crucial touchstone of titanic ambition, would be reduced to a passing episode. The entire structure and tragic import of the *Urfaust* was threatened by this change. None the less the younger German generation, for whom Goethe was already a national poet comparable only to Shakespeare and Dante, saw in the encyclopaedic outline of *Faust. A Fragment* an anticipation of their own schemes for an 'absolute' philosophy and a 'universal' poetry, and it was in these terms that the philosopher Schelling lectured on *Faust. A Fragment* in Jena in 1802.

For the Storm and Stress movement and its tragedies were obsolete in the 1790s. The German intelligentsia was shaken by newer and less personal passions. Every political and cultural certainty had been overturned by the French Revolution of 1789, and many saw a corresponding philosophical revolution in the work of Kant. Kant had investigated critically the productive role of the human mind in the construction of the world of our experience. In the Idealist philosophy of Fichte and other post-Kantians this critical programme was given a more uncompromising character, and the mind was made exclusively responsible for the world it inhabits. The role of Idealism in the intellectual ferment of Germany in the 1790s is difficult to overestimate. To the philosopher, such as Schelling or Hegel, it now seemed possible to achieve the ultimate goal of mapping out all possible knowledge; to the literary man such as Friedrich Schlegel it seemed rather that all experience could now be brought under the heading of literature, which was renamed 'Romantic poetry' and interpreted as the ultimately creative power of the human mind; to a theologian such as Schleiermacher the Idealist approach seemed to offer the possibility of a new justification for Christianity to a world grown pagan under the influence of the rationalist Enlightenment and the cult of ancient Greece and Rome.

Goethe was not a man to shut himself off from these movements, which deeply stirred his country, but he was far from sympathetic to any of them. When he returned to *Faust* in the period 1797 to 1801 he reversed his scheme of 1790 and decided that, although *Faust* would be extended by a second part, only the first part would for the present be completed, and its boundaries, and in particular its conclusion, would be no different from what had been intended in 1775. The character of Faust himself, though, without losing its links with the Storm and Stress period of Goethe's youth, would be enriched by the transcendental ambitions of the Idealist generation of the 1790s. This conscious incorporation of the material of his age into *Faust* made Goethe's relation with the play and its principal figure more intimate than with any other of his works except *Werther*, and this intimacy perhaps accounts for his difficulties in completing it. More than all his other works it was the expression of his lifelong and strenuous engagement with the thought and literature of his time. Perhaps he felt he owed it to himself, and to what had already been achieved, that he should add to it only the best – 'I could not be unworthy of myself, and so had to surpass myself', he wrote when the whole play was finished in 1831; and throughout his life he repeatedly affirmed in letters and conversations that his work on *Faust, Part Two* as well as *Part One*, was on the whole proceeding only a few lines at a time, the fruit of the mood of privileged moments. So close was *Faust* to the well-springs of Goethe's poetry that he may even have felt that he could not, as he once said, 'write the Amen' at the end of this work without drawing the line under his entire poetic career. Even three months before his death he was considering further additions to *Part Two*.

But for all the intimacy of the relation between the poem *Faust* and Goethe's life, Goethe is no more to be equated with the character Faust than he is with Werther. If Faust represents anything, he represents the temptations, offered by the contemporary intellectual and literary world, to which Goethe himself avoided succumbing – sometimes only narrowly. The same critical distance separates the author from the Storm and Stress hero of the *Urfaust* (e.g. the second *Street* scene, or *Dark Day, Countryside*) and from — in Goethe's phrase of 1816 — the 'abstrusely speculating' Idealist of the late 1790s (the two *Study* scenes). *Faust* is so closely connected with Goethe's life because it is in a sense a chronicle in which he drew up his reckoning with the changing cultural forces of his day by transforming them into poetry. Like *Wilhelm Meister's Years of Apprenticeship* — completed in 1796 — it is a work in which attitudes and beliefs which were once intended to furnish the key to the whole are preserved, as in amber, in the final version, where they appear as only partial interpretations, or even as pathological deviations, as stages along the route to a final goal, which itself may be only provisional.

Inevitably, since literary forms are themselves time-bound cultural products and the object of varying fashions, the lapse of time changed the form of *Faust*, as well as Goethe's intentions for its contents. Formally speaking, *Urfaust*, despite the novelty of its episodic structure, is a combination of two theatrical genres much in vogue in the 1770s — monodrama and domestic tragedy. But when Goethe wrote the *Urfaust*, every young avant-garde writer looked forward to the establishment of a German national theatre and thought it his patriotic duty to contribute plays to its repertoire. By about 1795 Goethe had recognised this pipe-dream for what it was, had written in *Wilhelm Meister* a literary epitaph on the theatre movement, and had himself largely given up writing plays. He could no longer write the most important work of which he was capable in a form in which he did not believe. He envisaged *Faust* now as a book to be read, an epic poem, say, rather than as a drama to be performed. In his choice of the sub-title 'Eine Tragödie' there may have been an allusion to Dante's epic poem, for the comparison of *Faust* with *The Divine Comedy* was commonplace in Idealist and Romantic circles around 1800. Of course *Faust* was to *contain* a drama, indeed a tragedy, for it was to contain the *Urfaust*, from which the dramatic, indeed tragic, effect was as inseparable as the expression of Storm and Stress yearnings. But that drama was to be enclosed in the amber of a new poetic medium; it was to be placed in a perspective that was more literary, more learned, more reflective, more lyrical. In working on *Part One* Goethe consulted earlier versions of the Faust legend and multiplied allusions to them in his text — his Faust and Mephistopheles now seem occasionally to know that there have been other Fausts and Mephistopheles before them. Sometimes there are poetic intrusions on the dramatic illusion, and neither the length of the speeches nor the number of the characters is kept within the limits of theatrical practicality (e.g. *Walpurgis Night*). Most important of all, the enlarged scheme of the play involved the construction of a reflective framework around the principal action: while the action itself, in *Part One* and *Part Two*, was to be tragic in character, the framework, in meditating on the action, was to offer the hope of a resolution and transfiguration of the tragic catastrophe. Goethe had already attempted such resolutions at the end of his dramas *Egmont* and *Tasso* by a deliberate transition from a dramatic to a lyrical mode. *Faust* too was, in 1800, planned to begin and end with the solitary voice of the musing poet, though of this plan only the opening poem, 'Dedication', was retained.

How, then, are we to read *Faust*? Taken as a whole, the framework and the two parts together, it is a dramatic poem — rather than simply a play — which grew in time along with the movements it depicts. It is a many-layered work which offers us, in the context of a meditation on human life and destiny, a poetic, and partially dramatic, representation of half a century of the life of the European mind by a uniquely gifted, and unusually well-placed, observer. It is best understood as an epic as Ezra Pound defined the genre — a 'poem including history' — and in writing it Goethe successfully realised the ambition Pound set himself, but failed to achieve, in *Cantos*: in Hugh Kenner's words, 'to become, while writing the poem in public, the poet capable of ending it'.

The question how we are to read *Faust. Part One* is easier

to answer. Goethe in the end treated *Urfaust*, that miraculous
product of his own poetic springtime, with great gentleness,
and in expanding it into *Part One* altered its structure very little. *Part One* is still performable, and it is still − just − a
tragedy. The meditative and poetic incursions are not disrup-
tive, not even in the last scene. We must, however, follow
Goethe's instructions precisely: the title-pages in all editions
authorised by Goethe make it plain that *Faust. Part One*
begins where *Urfaust* began, with the *Night* scene and with
Faust sitting in his study. The preliminary material, the poem
Dedication, the *Prelude on the Stage* and − particularly
− the *Prologue in Heaven*, are constituents of the encom-
passing lyrical framework and no more belong to *Part One*
than does *Part Two*. Artificial problems in the interpretation
of *Faust. Part One* are created when the critic includes in his
discussion scenes, such as the *Prologue in Heaven* or Faust's
death in *Part Two*, which are assigned by Goethe to quite different places, and quite different functions, in the whole
work.

The principal tensions in *Part One* are identical with the
principal tensions in *Urfaust*, which has, and needs, no *Prologue* and no *Part Two*. They are tensions still largely
dramatic and still rooted in the scenes which show us Faust's
earthly life and his understanding, or misunderstanding, of its
purpose: can life be lived as Faust wishes to live it, and what
is the consequence − in *this* world − of making the attempt?
These questions are resolved, not originated, in the visionary
and mainly ironic scenes located in the heavenly realms. To
base an interpretation of *Faust* on the *Prologue in Heaven*
would be to imply that God and the Devil are the principal
actors in a play which is actually *about* the life of a man in
a non-theological age. To *start* an interpretation with that
scene would be to misrepresent as being the first step in the
plot what is actually a vision of the world order for which only the play as a whole can provide the justification. On this
earth, and in this life, which are all we know, and all the
modern poet can directly represent, the Faustian tensions end

in tragedy. To interpret the whole of *Faust* cannot be our principal purpose here. Provided we begin and end where Goethe tells us to, we may read *Faust. Part One* as a tragic drama.

The 'framework' of *Faust. A Tragedy*

Dedication (Zueignung)	autobiographical	
Prelude on the Stage		
(Vorspiel auf dem Theater)	aesthetic	} introdu
Prologue in Heaven (Prolog		
im Himmel)	metaphysical	
Part One		
Part Two (to Faust's death)		
Deposition (Grablegung)	satirical	
Mountain Chasms		} epilogue
(Bergschluchten)	mystical	

Faust. Part One: **Synopsis of contents**

Note. An asterisk * indicates a scene present in *Urfaust*; a bracket asterisk (*) indicates a scene partially present in *Urfaust*; the dagger † indicates that *Urfaust* has here the additional scene *High Road* (*Landstrasse*).

SCENE	EVENTS
(*) *Night (Nacht)*	*Monologue; *Spirit of Earth; *Wagner; suicide attempt
Outside the Gates (Vor dem Tor)	Walk with Wagner, evil spirits summoned
Study (Studierzimmer) I	Mephistopheles materialises
(*) *Study (Studierzimmer) II*	Curse; Wager; *student
* *Auerbach's Cellar in Leipzig (Auerbachs Keller in Leipzig)*†	'Merrymaking'
Witch's Kitchen (Hexenküche)	Faust rejuvenated
* *Street (Strasse)*	Faust meets Gretchen
* *Evening (Abend)*	Jewels hidden and found, 'King in Thule'
* *Promenade (Spaziergang)*	Jewels confiscated
* *The Neighbour's House (Der Nachbarin Haus)*	Second gift of jewels, Martha's husband's 'death'
* *Street (Strasse)*	Faust agrees to lie
* *Garden (Garten)*	Conversations: Martha, Mephistopheles, Gretchen, Faust
* *A Summerhouse (Ein Gartenhäuschen)*	First kiss
(*) *Forest, Cavern (Wald und Hohle)*	Monologue; *decision to return
* *Gretchen's Room (Gretchens Stube)*	Spinning-wheel song

* *Martha's Garden (Marthens Garten)*	Conversation on religion, tryst
* *At the Well (Am Brunnen)*	Gossip
* *Town Wall, Alley (Zwinger)*	Prayer to Virgin
(*) *Night (Nacht)*	*Valentin's monologue; Valentin killed
* *Cathedral (Dom)*	Gretchen swoons
Walpurgis Night (Walpurgisnacht)	Faust on Brocken
Walpurgis Night's Dream (Walpurgisnachtstraum)	Satire (Gretchen forgotten)
* *Dark Day, Countryside (Trüber Tag. Feld)*	Faust's guilt, rescue resolved
* *Night, Open Country (Nacht. Offen Feld)*	Gibbet
* *Prison (Kerker)*	Gretchen's madness and renunciation

Chapter 2

A modern Faust

(Night – Outside the Gates)

*Alone in his study on Easter Saturday night, Faust, longing
to embrace the source of all life, turns to a book of magic.
Its image of the Macrocosm seems too abstract, but then the
Earth Spirit, summoned up by a spell, overpowers him completely. A conversation with his assistant Wagner leaves Faust
convinced that only suicide offers him the possibility of new
life. As Easter Day dawns, however, the memory of the
Christian faith of his childhood moves him to put aside the
poison he has prepared. Later in the day Faust and Wagner
join the townsfolk walking out into the spring landscape.
Faust is hailed by the country people as a benefactor who
once saved many lives during an outbreak of plague. Still
unconvinced of the value of learning Faust calls on the spirits
of the air to help him escape from his present existence. A
black dog appears which Faust summons to accompany him
back into town.*

The scene *Night* was composed at two very different times in
Goethe's life. Lines *354–605* (Penguin 43–51, Everyman
13–21) were probably written in 1773 or a little earlier, lines
606–807 (P52–7, E21–7) probably in 1799–1800. Despite dif-
ferences in style, the two sections are integrated into a single,
regular dramatic pulse. Storm and Stress passes easily, and,
for most readers, imperceptibly, into 1790s Idealism.

Like the opening scene of any Faust play, *Night* has the
greatest structural importance for the play as a whole. It has
both to expound the principal themes and to initiate the
action. But it has also a symbolic and architectural role. The
night in question is the night of Holy Saturday, when Christ

25

lay dead in the tomb. The dead hour in which the play begins not only underlines its essentially post-Christian setting: there is also a foreshadowing of the midnight hour at which Faust himself will die at the end of *Part Two*. Nothing in Goethe is ever static, however, and as this night wears on to morning so it anticipates, firstly and more nearly, its own tragic parody in the night that passes into a drear dawn in the last scene of *Part One*, and then, more remotely, the sunrise that opens *Part Two* and even the 'new day' of the last scene of all, into which Faust is once again introduced by a chorus of angels.

The internal structure of the scene, moreover, establishes a pattern that will give shape to all Faust's subsequent experiences: a first state of inertia and constriction is followed by a crescendo of emotion which culminates in a moment of creativity and vision, followed by interruption and relapse. This pattern, three times repeated in *Night*, is resumed in *Outside the Gates* to reach a fourth culmination two scenes later in Faust's agreement with Mephistopheles. A further, even more extended, repetition, with its own subordinate climaxes, takes us from the agreement with the Devil to the end of the Gretchen story and, with it, of *Part One*.

Goethe himself described *Night* as a 'monodrama'. It is decisive for both the form and content of the play *Faust* that it begins with a man alone, in the company only of his ambition and of a series of visions. Faust is cut off from the rest of humanity and from nature, for it is night, and from activity, for he is indoors. The play will tell us the story of Faust's attempted journey from solitude into natural and human community, and in the form *par excellence* of solitude the monologue. *Faust* will thus become, like Hegel' *Phenomenology of Mind* (1807), the explicitly modern story of an explicitly modern consciousness. Like so many founder of modern European culture – like Luther, also in his study alone with the Devil, like Montaigne in his library, like Descartes in his 'stove' – Faust begins alone in a room. Let us consider the nature of the ambition with which he is closeted.

From that self-imposed isolation Faust longs to *escape* (*417*). The longing to break out of his room is the theatrical and poetic image of a longing to break out of the isolation of being himself. But it is not simply release that Faust is looking for. He wants to break out *into a world* (*382, 409, 464*) – into a beyond of things and people that will keep him company, even if he has at the moment only the most indefinite notion of what they might be: a ghostly landscape illuminated by the moon (*392–7*), indeterminate spirits with whom one might communicate (*394, 425*). This impetus, from the self out into the world, is a theme in a certain kind of European philosophy from Descartes' *Discourse on Method* (1637) to Fichte's *On the Vocation of Man* (1800), and it was under intense discussion in Germany in the last years of the eighteenth century, at the very time when Goethe was turning *Urfaust* into *Faust. Part One*. German Idealist philosophy of this period sought to reconstruct the order of the world by starting from the order of the individual reflective mind, and to some extent Faust's ambition is a poetical version of that ambition of the philosophers. But of course Faust, as he tells us in his first line, has had enough of philosophy. He wants the world into which he breaks out to be, not the mere idea or thought of a world, but a world *that is alive* (*414, 456*), alive as he is. He wants, that is, the world to be not just opposed to or different from him, but to share in something of his own inmost identity as a living being. And in this lies the beginning of what we may call his tragic flaw. For in this first scene, as throughout his life, Faust does not seek an escape into, or a relation with, a world independent of him, and of which he is only a part. The world will be alive for him only in so far as it will share in *his* life. He wants to enjoy, and to communicate with, this world and its every part, but he does not envisage this process as in any way transforming himself (*382–5, 455, 464–7*). He wants to break into a world, but he does not want to lose himself in doing so. In the terminology of the older Goethe, Faust – and with him perhaps an entire strand in the European cultural tradition of which he is the poetic representative – does not know how to 'renounce'.

Lines 354–429 (P43–5, E13–15)

Goethe presents his hero to us in the closest association with his traditional origins. An audience expects an opening monologue of any Faust, even a 'new' one. For this episode, traditional since the sixteenth century, Goethe uses a verse-form which for his readers was associated with the earthy popular culture of sixteenth-century Germany: the *Knittelvers* or doggerel, much used by the Mastersinger Hans Sachs and imitated by Goethe in the 1770s in a number of humorous poems and semi-farcical dramatic sketches. Each line has four stresses, but the pattern of unstressed syllables is irregular, and the lines usually rhyme as couplets. (For example,

> Hábe nun, aćh! Phílosophíe,
> Júristeréi und Médiziń.

The first four lines of *Part One* (but not of *Urfaust*) are unusual in rhyming as a quatrain, not as couplets.) What Faust says, too, is harmonious with a sixteenth-century setting: the faculties in which he has studied – philosophy, law, medicine and theology – are those of the early modern university. Rabelais would approve of his satirical allusions to the empty formalism of academic knowledge, and his ambitions, for land, money and reputation (*374–5*), would be comprehensible to Marlowe. The method he chooses to escape from his frustration is the occult knowledge, white magic, or *pansophia*, that fascinated Cornelius Agrippa, Paracelsus, Jakob Böhme, and also more respectable figures, such as Kepler: an active understanding, at once scientific and mystical, of the harmonious nature of all creation (*382–5*). Even Faust's confession that he is an unbeliever in religious matters is expressed in a downright, picturesque way that is unaffected by seventeenth- or eighteenth-century scepticism (*368–9*), though even these lines contain no direct defiance of God. In the play's opening words we recognise a traditional sixteenth-century Dr Faustus who has already taken the decision to devote himself to magic but has not yet started to use the occult sciences for his own benefit.

However, a drastic change in tonality now occurs (386), and suddenly this Faust seems as much an eighteenth-century figure as a figure from the Renaissance or Reformation. The *Knittelvers* − which is actually quite rare in *Faust* − gives way to what will be by far the predominant verse-form of the play, the 'madrigal verse'. In this line the number of stresses may vary, but there is a regular alternation of stressed and unstressed syllables, e.g.

O sähst du, vóller Móndenschéin,

while the rhyming patterns are very varied, the simple couplet usually being avoided. This fluent form, seen at its best, outside *Faust*, in Wieland's *Tales in Verse*, is, as its name implies, particularly suited for arias and recitative in opera − supremely the eighteenth-century art. And what Faust now says, in this new form, is also conceivable only in the eighteenth century: he turns to the moon, his 'mournful friend', the noun suggesting the friendship-cult of the Sentimentalist poet Klopstock, the adjective suggesting a landscape such as that of Goethe's own poem 'Welcome and Farewell' (1771). With references to caverns, meadows and dew, Faust's sensibility is now that of a man of the 1770s.

There is nevertheless a seamless continuity with what has gone before. Even though the verse is madrigal verse, the rhyming continues in four-stressed couplets, as in the *Knittelvers*, and does not give way to quatrains and more complicated patterns until line 401. In the picture of Faust dancing with spirits in the moonlight (392–7) there are not only echoes of those eighteenth-century cult-figures Swedenborg and Ossian, there are also perhaps reminiscences of sixteenth- and seventeenth-century representations of the witches' sabbath. And the central opening theme of Faust's ambition, though significantly enlarged, is not fundamentally changed. Already in the *Knittelvers* monologue Faust had expressed a desire for the most intimate knowledge of the workings of the universe, rather than a mere rummaging in words (382–5), a phrase which with true Renaissance confidence dismisses medieval Christian culture *en bloc*. Now, in the paragraph from *386* to *397*, he seeks in his imagination an identity with the moonlight. The sensual associations of being surrounded and washed over by this element become more prominent (the word 'in' recurs three times), as does the implicit imagery of water. The violent contrast provided in the next paragraph (*398–409*) by the imagery of dust and dryness characterising Faust's study resumes that earlier contrast between intimacy and mere words, in an extensive development of synonyms for 'rummage'. Even though the references to the manuscripts and instruments piled up around him keep us aware of the nominal setting of the scene in a sixteenth-century humanist scholar's study, the expression of personal frustration, the appeal to the heart, to Nature (*414*) as the divinely ordained, deeply sensual complement to man – this is a perspective on the human condition possible only to a sophisticated eighteenth-century mind. Yet it is a continuous, logical and rhetorical, development of an anguish and ambition originally expressed by a figure who, as verse-form, scene-setting, name and his naive dramatic self-presentation show, comes from a puppet-play or chap-book of two centuries before. Within sixty lines Goethe has established this figure as the vehicle for the deepest and most personal yearnings of his age, and has thereby established the broad historical milieu within which the result of the play will move. Goethe will freely mingle elements from his contemporary eighteenth-century world, to which his play belongs and which it is about, with elements from the sixteenth-century world in which the theme was born and the story received its first articulation. The – necessarily self-conscious – non-chronological intermingling of historical elements which is carried to an extreme in *Faust. Part Two* (*7433*) is already present in *Part One*.

Faust exhorts himself to escape from his prison (*418*). And so his tragic flaw begins to take effect, so his decline begins from the innocence of his original yearning for a world of life. Because he derives his notion of what that world might be not from the world that actually surrounds him – mere 'rummage' – but from the 'life' of his inner self, Faust's yearning for it becomes contaminated by turns with subjectivity, negativity, perversity and, ultimately, moral evil. In the remainder of this scene three attempts will be made, of increasing length and complexity, to achieve by unnatural, that is, magical, means the escape into a living world which Faust's natural existence denies, or appears to deny him: his vision of the macrocosmic order, his conjuring of the Spirit of Earth, and his attempt at suicide.

Lines 430–59 (P45–6, E15–16)

Early works of astronomy, or works of alchemy or magic such as those Goethe is known to have studied in 1769–70, often contained a schematic or symbolic representation of the order of the universe, of the spheres of the heavens, all emanating from the Holy Trinity, and each associated with a planet, a chemical element and some more or less mysterious sign. In such a schema, the 'sign of the macrocosm', Faust recognises a picture of the union of God and Nature, the goal of his ambition (*441* cp. *384*). The sign seems of divine origin and arouses in Faust a feeling of his own divinity (*434, 439*). But his contemplation is abruptly broken off as Faust realises that this experience is 'only' (*454*) contemplation, not living union. He rejects, that is, the mere *sign* of the totality he wishes to embrace, and this rejection of any mediation of experience through representation – particularly through representation in language – will be characteristic of him throughout the play. The image of dryness returns (*458–9*) and with it Faust's original frustration.

Lines 460–517 (P46–8, E16–18)

Faust's second attempt to achieve his goal follows the same pattern as the previous episode. In an introductory section he reacts to the new sign, that of the Spirit of Earth, and the emotional tension rises as, after some insistent rhyming, the play for the first time breaks into irregular free verse, rhyme being only gradually restored as Faust decides to summon up the spirit. In a further formal intensification, monologue for the first time gives way to dialogue, marking a progression in Faust's experience, but the dialogue proves only a confrontation of unequals and Faust is returned to despair.

The question 'who or what is the Spirit of Earth?' is best answered, not by investigating the possible cabbalistic sources of the name, but by considering the relation of this scene to the traditional format of the Faust play, and to the themes of this particular Faust play that have so far emerged. If we compare the opening of Goethe's *Faust* with the opening of the chap-book, of Marlowe's *Doctor Faustus*, or of the puppet plays, the scene with the Spirit of Earth clearly corresponds to the scenes in which the earlier Faust summons up the Devil – sometimes specifically Lucifer, sometimes a preliminary incarnation of Mephistopheles – but, finding him too hideous or terrifying, has recourse instead to a more amenable manifestation. Just as Goethe's Faust is a 'new' Faust for an eighteenth-century audience, so the Spirit of Earth is a 'new' devil for an age whose intellectuals at least could not take seriously the old one. For Goethe, as for Kant, and indeed for the whole Enlightenment, moral evil is a human, not a cosmic phenomenon. The Spirit of Earth is beyond good and evil, a power of which Mephistopheles, the specific embodiment of evil, who is to accompany Faust throughout his career, can appear to be an emanation. But the Spirit of Earth is not only the most nearly diabolical, he is also the most nearly divine power a modern man like Faust can invoke. For, turning to what Goethe has so far shown us of the expression and frustration of Faust's ambition, we can say that the Spirit of Earth is, like the sign of the macrocosm, a representation for Faust of all there is. But he represents the universe, not as a mere sign 'lying before the mind' (*441*), but as a living being with whom it is possible for another living being to converse – three times the Spirit associates himself with the word 'life' (*501, 507, 509*). For this reason Faust feels 'nearer' to him than to the sign of the macrocosm (*461*).

Throughout the dialogue, however, there is manifest an inequality in the partners. On the one hand Faust asserts his own comparability with the Spirit (*500, 511*) – indeed, remembering he is made in the image of God, he claims, with characteristic hyperbole, to be even greater than the Spirit of Earth, who merely constructs the Godhead's material garment (*516–17, 509*), i.e. the physical world. On the other hand, Faust's ambition to be identified with the world process, as the Spirit of Earth is identified with it, proves absurdly overweening once the manifestation of the Spirit reveals to him and us what it would be like for that ambition to be achieved. Faust's own evocation of the contradictory features of life, into which he is prepared to venture (*464–8*), is quite overshadowed by the Spirit's sinister chant, with its relentless sequence of antitheses, which does not even acknowledge Faust's presence (*501–9*). Faust can no more encompass the Spirit of Earth, can no more live the life of the whole material universe, than he can gaze into the sun.

But the Spirit of Earth, as he vanishes, does not leave Faust without all consolation. Faust is himself a spirit, if not the spirit of the whole world, and if he wishes to realise his ambition of grasping and experiencing the life of the world he may do so in a way and at a spiritual level appropriate to the particular human being that he is:

> Du gleichst dem Geist, den du begreifst,
> Nicht mir!   (*513–13*)

(You match the spirit you can grasp, not me!)

– lines which express not only contempt but also, it is often held, a promise of the coming of Mephistopheles. Faust's first two visions were premature fulfilments, short circuits, of his unnatural ambition to live in a world that is infinitely rich and full and yet also wholly his own. Only by a magical, an unnatural way can that ambition be fulfilled. The way, however, must be proportionate to the human being who treads it, and the spirit that accompanies Faust will have a human form and often look very like Faust himself. But it will be Faust's perversity never to acknowledge this spirit of moral evil, of cosmic negativity on the human scale, for what it is, and even now the hint uttered by the Spirit of Earth passes him by.

Lines 518–601 (P48–51, E18–21)

The semi-comic dialogue with Wagner returns us to the cruel banality of Faust's human starting-point: a location which is more clearly that of a sixteenth-century German university than anything we have seen since the play's opening lines. Since Wagner's own ambition is not in a sense very different from Faust's (cp. *382* and *586–7*; *456* and *563*), we see in him an image of what Faust would become without his recourse to magic. Moreover, the opposition between words and the feelings they express, which is the subject of the conversation, takes up the theme of hostility to signs, which we have already noticed in the Macrocosm scene. But the principal function of the episode is of course to be a comic interlude, and, as the first of many such abrupt reversals of mood, it completes our introduction to the poetical scope of the drama: its sixteenth-century roots and its eighteenth-century context; its metrical variety, from *Knittelvers* to free verse; its fusion of philosophical profundity and satirical levity; its emotional range from ecstasy through despair and bitterness to sardonic, even farcical humour; its dramatic range from impassioned monologue to ironical banter.

Lines 602–807 (P51–7, E21–7)

In the second half of *Night* the flaw, the unnatural quality, in Faust's ambition is demonstrated at length. Because that ambition is based on a denial, a denial of the conditions in which ordinary people lead ordinary lives and so come into possession of their ordinary worlds, it is now shown to lead him to the brink of suicide, the ultimate negation – or short-circuit – of natural experience. The motif of Faust's suicide attempt is original to Goethe, and we may be sure that Goethe had a far-reaching structural intention in introducing it. Everything Faust undertakes after this scene, the entire life he chooses to live, is marked out as, for him, the next-best thing to suicide, the most negative form of existence short of actual self-destruction.

The historical perspective also is broadened and deepened. Faust has been introduced to us as a sixteenth-century scholar, full of the explosive speculative energies of the new Renaissance learning and the Reformation in religion, and to some extent those energies have been recognisably translated into the language of the 1770s, the age of Sentimentalism and the age of genius. In this second half of *Night* Faust's revolt against his intellectual inheritance is no longer merely a part of his traditional characterisation, nor is it merely a simile for the revolt of young men in the 1770s. It is now a representation of the general condition of life in an age in which that inheritance has lost its power, in which Christian categories have ceased to supply the philosophical, juridical, emotional and moral framework for everyday existence. The moral challenge of the great process of secularisation, which had advanced so far among eighteenth-century German intellectuals, is represented in a story which emerges from the Reformation period, in which that process was just beginning. Faust now gradually ceases to regard himself as exceptional by virtue of his individual genius. Instead, Faust sees himself as the modern man who lives − that is, who rejects suicide − unsupported by the beliefs of the man of the past. Faust defines himself, in fact, as post-Christian.

Now and in the three scenes to come, Faust's original longing for a world of living experience declines further into a passionate negativity, whose theological expression is certainly indebted to Romantic and Idealist speculation of the 1790s. Goethe is beginning to specify the new words and new concepts in which a modern Faust can bind himself to the Devil. But Goethe is also preparing to raise the story of Faust and Gretchen, which will then follow, to the level of a paradigm: in that story he will define by means of a classic example what it is to be modern, to be precisely a *new* Faust, not the Faust of the old story. *Faust. Part One* will thus become the tragedy not just of exceptional genius, not just of the individualist literary intellectual, but of post-Christian man, of self-conscious modernity − the tragedy of Europe in Goethe's time, which is after all in many respects, and perhaps particularly in this one, continuous with our own.

After Wagner has left, Faust recalls the despair from which this interruption rescued him (602–29) and quails at the thought of the deadening weight of care which presses down on the life of the ordinary, natural man (630–51 cp. 11384–498). The imagery of dust, applied to the contents of his room, establishes a continuity with his earlier speeches, as Faust denounces intellectual traditions that are merely inherited and not recreated anew by each generation (656–85). Having thus discarded the support of the past, and unwilling to stupefy himself with the anxieties of everyday existence, Faust, in full clarity, and complete isolation, faces what Camus has called the ultimate philosophical question. It is a question which Goethe had assiduously avoided since he gave it classic, and for his age overwhelming, expression in *The Sorrows of Young Werther*: has life anything to offer the feeling heart that might dissuade it from suicide? That question, already foreshadowed in lines 386–7, is the point of departure for Faust's odyssey, and no answer will be given until the moment of the agreement with Mephistopheles. The answer that emerges for the present is therefore intentionally provisional, being both dramatically and intellectually unconvincing: Faust escapes suicide only instinctively, and by allowing himself to be swayed by memories of a religion in which he no longer believes.

The phial of poison is the first treacherous substitute for what Faust has outgrown, seeming to promise him the release from constriction and into a new life for which he yearned (689 cp. 392–3), and suddenly the imagery of dust and desiccation is replaced by that of water and the sea (698–701). Emphasising that this is exclusively his chosen action, his *acte gratuit* (734), Faust puts the poison, in a festal cup, to his lips. But an angelic chorus, singing of Christ's atoning passion and resurrection holds him back from death, even though he can give no explicit, metaphorical or poetic reason why it should.

The angels' message is not for him, he says, but for other more sensitive, perhaps weaker, souls (*764*),

> Die Botschaft hör' ich wohl, allein mir fehlt der Glaube. (*765*)

(I hear the message, but I lack the faith.)

This famous line anticipates a whole century of German attempts to formulate the message, or 'essence', of Christianity independently of its miraculous (*766*) origins. And the rest of *Faust* will be devoted to the search for a reason why suicide is not necessary, a reason in which it is possible for a post-Christian man to believe. Faust himself will never do, more than glimpse that reason because he lacks the willingness, possessed for example by Goethe, to renounce his claim to absolute self-determination and to accept the gift of his life of love and beauty. Goethe here identifies the essentially historical nature of this, his tragic theme. The theme concerns not humanity in general, but the human race at and after a particular moment in its history, the moment when it has ceased to be Christian, when the Easter message can act upon it only as something in which it *once* believed, only as a memory of childhood (*781–2*). Faust at this stage speaks like a pagan German intellectual of the late eighteenth century – like Friedrich Schlegel or Schelling, or like one aspect of Goethe himself – while the angels sing with the seductive voices of the new apologists for Christianity, Schleiermacher and Novalis (whose essay, *Christendom, or Europe*, with which the last chorus of angels shows some parallels, Goethe read in December 1799). Faust listens to that siren song and is not convinced – but he sees the point.

It is suggested sometimes that the choruses of angels, women and disciples must be interpreted as the voices of participants in a liturgical play at a nearby church. This unnecessary assumption fails to take account of the mixture of genres in the dramatic poem *Faust*, which has at this point itself become something like a liturgical play or oratorio. What Faust hears is the voice of historical Christianity, another vision in his long night of monologue. If Goethe were constructing a drama in which effects follow on causes in a single plane of material and psychological reality, there would be a contradiction between Faust's acknowledgement of the heavenly origin of the choruses (*762, 767–8*) and his refusal to believe them. But Goethe is here presenting symbols of conflicting forces to the mind of the reader of his poem.

Lines 808–948 (P57–62, E27–32)

The choruses and the dawn already have established a mood of celebration, but there is still a powerful contrast between the solitude of the first scene, unrelieved in its later part, and the sudden explosion of multifarious social existence in the opening of *Outside the Gates*. We are plunged into the small-town world of artisans, apprentices and respectable burghers all out for an Easter Sunday walk, the world of provincial – perhaps particularly Catholic – Germany at any time from the sixteenth to the nineteenth century, with its little love-affairs, its soldiers and fortune-tellers: the world, in fact, of Gretchen. The Gretchen story is also foreshadowed in the formal structure Goethe adopts: the snatches of conversation intermingling with songs, and the counterpointing of romance and satire. We are given, too, a first glimpse of Faust's relationship to Gretchen's milieu: against the background of variegated song and dialogue his own monologue stands out with all the intransigence of an alienated individualist. True, he breathes deeply of the fresh air of spring and of human company and, unlike his companion Wagner (*941–8*), he acknowledges that here, amid innocent and natural human beings, is where he belongs (*940* cp. *11407*). But Faust cannot himself be one of these happy if limited beings: he is separated from them by the power of his own reflection, by the very fact that he thinks about them as they do not think about him, by everything that has passed before our eyes in the scene *Night.* Above all, there is his religious position: Faust does not share their untroubled faith and so he can see the social, even anthropological, function which faith serves:

> Sie feiern die Auferstehung des Herrn,
> Denn sie sind selber auferstanden.   (*921–2*)

(They are celebrating the rising of the Lord because they themselves have risen again.)

As later, in the Gretchen story, religion here provides the symbol and the occasion of Faust's separation from traditional and conventional social life.

Lines 949–1067 (P62–6, E32–5)

The scene shifts as Faust and Wagner walk on (937) to a nearby village. Here the peasants gather round to pay their respects, and offer refreshment, to the learned doctor who in his youth assisted his father in bringing healing to the plague-stricken countryside. Faust courteously accepts their tribute and utters the pieties appropriate to one of his class and education (1009–10). But though he thus symbolically drinks the cup of life from the hand of human society, rather than the cup of death he proffered himself in solitude the night before, he shows no gratitude. Faust – now characterised, incidentally, as a man of middle age and much experience – is so distrustful of all his inherited learning that even his father's altruistic and apparently beneficial application of science seems to him the work of an alchemist, whose medicaments were more deadly than the plague. His corrosive negativity leaves him impervious both to the angels' exhortation to apostolic charity (801–5) and to Wagner's more prosaic belief in the value of dutifully, if uncomprehendingly, accumulated knowledge (1056–63).

Lines 1068–141 (P66–8, E35–7)

Having cut himself off from society and its religion, Faust is once more spiritually as alone as he was during his solitary vigil. The negative component of his ambition, the desire to escape, is coming increasingly to predominate over the positive vision of an endlessly living world to be appropriated. The sun is now low in the sky, and in a speech of great imaginative power Faust utters a desire for wings to fly on in endless pursuit of it, westering round the world for ever.

This immensely suggestive image of endless enjoyment con-
joined with endless unfulfilment expresses more than Faust's
yearning to escape from the confines of the world he has been
born into and where he believes he can achieve nothing. It
expresses also the unnatural and paradoxical character of that
yearning: the seas he imagines himself winging across are like
the 'mirroring tide' (700) which sparkled at him in his study
from the phial of poison; physically (1091) they are as inaccessible as if they could be reached only by death. The
paradox goes deeper. It seems to be in the nature of Faust's
capacity for wishing that it should drive him beyond what
reality offers, for one does not wish for what one possesses
already. He appears to be born in order that he should always
wish and always be frustrated (1090–3).

This paradox within Faust's own nature means nothing to
Wagner, whose ambitions are purely intellectual and do not
extend to the material world, and Faust reformulates the
paradox in a famous speech (1112–17). The boundless aspira-
tion, already expressed by Faust in the monologue which
opened the play, has two aspects: on the one hand it is a drive
to enjoy in love all that there is; on the other hand it is a drive
to reject violently any given reality in the interests of an
enjoyment that lies beyond it. The spirit of love for what he
has not causes Faust to reject what he has, and the spirit of
rejection is simply the negative image and consequence of the
spirit of love. Faust's intuition that these two spirits are about
to separate is prophetic: the spirit of rejection in him will
shortly take on a separate existence in the shape of
Mephistopheles, whose materialisation is about to begin.

For once again, on finding himself frustrated by nature –
this time, his own nature – Faust turns his thoughts to
magic. He yearns for a magic cloak, the 'bodily wings' (1091)
with which nature will not provide him and which could carry
him off into foreign lands and a new life. This magic cloak,
which will be a leitmotif throughout both parts of the play,
and the provision of which is one of the few tangible benefits
Faust has from his association with Mephistopheles, is the
image of the realisation of his unnatural wishes – such as,

particularly, the desire to be somewhere other than where he is. In the hope that they may furnish him with such a cloak, Faust, to Wagner's alarm, invokes the evil spirits, the spirits of the air.

Lines 1142–77 (P68–9, E37–8)

The sun has now set and dusk is falling. Faust sees a black dog circling around himself and Wagner, and immediately his thoughts leap to the possibility that the dog is a spirit seeking a magical hold over him (*1158–9*). His unspoken intentions are revealed by his commanding the dog to join him none the less (*1166*) and by his disappointment when no preternatural consequences seem to follow. After some strenuous emotional passages the scene has ended as light-heartedly as it began, even though Faust has now, and wittingly, taken his first steps towards a pact with the Devil.

Chapter 3

The wager

(Study I — Study II — Auerbach's Cellar in Leipzig —
Witch's Kitchen)*

*Faust, back in his study, begins translating St John. The dog
changes into Mephistopheles, who hints at a pact, plunges
Faust into sensual dreams, and departs. On Mephistopheles'
return, Faust curses the world, denying that it contains
anything good. Mephistopheles cynically counters that, like
everyone else, Faust will eventually find it satisfying enough.
Faust wagers that, whatever the Devil gives him, he will never
be so content with any single moment of his life that he could
wish that moment prolonged. Mephistopheles agrees to serve
Faust and show him everything the world can offer. After
Mephistopheles, impersonating Faust, has given treacherous
advice to an enquiring freshman, the two fly off to a hostelry.
The middle-aged Faust, unimpressed by merry-making, is
now taken to a witch's kitchen where he drinks a rejuvenating
potion and has a vision of perfect female beauty.*

The first *Study* scene is in some ways a continuation or reprise
of the play's opening: at night in his study Faust yearns for
the watery sources of life (*1200–1*), opens a spiritually significant book (*1217*), meets a supernatural force and is granted
an ecstatic, if deceitful, vision, from which he awakens disap-
pointed 'once more' (*1526*). Although the drama progresses
decisively, in that Faust at last begins a permanent dialogue
with the magical world, represented now by Mephistopheles

---

*   In the Penguin edition the direction *Faust's Study (i)* is incorrectly added
to the title of the opening scene *Night*. The scenes universally known as *Study
I* and *Study II* are in that edition therefore numbered *Study (ii)* and *Study
(iii)*.

it is clear by the end of the scene that this dialogue is doomed to be permanently unrewarding. We are taken to the point at which traditionally Faust would have made his pact, and shown why the old kind of agreement cannot catch the imagination of a 'modern' man. The scene is therefore suffused with literary artificiality and self-consciousness.

Lines 1178–1237 (P70–1, E39–40)

Faust travels a long way in *Study I*. He begins enclosed in the peaceful Christian certainties of the love of God and man (*1184–5*), which he will never know again and which are reflected in the stable stanzaic form (*1178–85, 1194–1201*). This form, however, is gradually disrupted, at first in rhythm, then in rhyme, by the interventions of the dog (*1186–93, 1202–9*). But even the unquiet yearnings of the mystic (*1200–1, 1212–13*) have their place in traditional piety, and when Faust, unable to regain inner peace, turns to an external source of divine revelation in the New Testament, he is still the – fundamentally Christian – Renaissance humanist scholar he was introduced to us as. But Goethe's Faust does not spend long in the role of Martin Luther, Germany's greatest translator of the Bible, and an almost exact contemporary of the historical Faust. We are reminded of the sixteenth-century roots of the story – and of the sixteenth-century *Knittelvers* – in the very moment in which Faust's consciousness is most emphatically shown to be that of a late-eighteenth-century intellectual. For Faust's scholarship is modelled not on that of Luther but on the by-products of the rise of modern biblical criticism, on the rationalist rewriting of the Scriptures by such as Lorenz Schmidt or C. F. Bahrdt, whom Goethe had already satirised in a skit of 1774.

In his successive attempts at rendering the first words of St John's Gospel Faust recapitulates his own development towards explicit modernity in *Night*: he refuses to define his origin and goal either as a 'word' (*1225* cp. *385*), or as the 'meaning' of all things, offered by the macrocosmic sign (*1229*), or as the 'power' which he glimpsed in the Spirit of

Earth but in which he could not share (*1233*). Only by asserting that 'in the beginning was the deed' (*1237*) does Faust do justice to the desire that has moved him from the start of the play and that lured him on to the 'pure activity' of suicide at the end of *Night* (*705, 712*): the desire to discover, at the centre of the living force that creates all things (*1232*), something identical with himself. For 'deed' implies not only the fulfilment that 'power' merely promises, but also a doer. In thus identifying the heart of living nature with the heart of human nature Faust has advanced to a position similar to that of Goethe's Idealist contemporary, the reputedly atheist Fichte. Fichte saw the ultimate certainty of philosophy as lying not in some mere fact (*Tatsache*) that was known, but in an act or 'factition' (*Tathandlung*) by which the reflecting self posited its own existence.

Like the speaker in Fichte's *On the Vocation of Man*, or like the reader of Hegel's encyclopaedic works, Faust is assisted to this insight into the nature of things by the intervention of a 'spirit' (*1236*). For the philosophers that 'spirit' is but a synonym for the active human consciousness. For Faust it is almost certainly 'the great spirit' that has appeared to him (cp. *1746, 3217–19, Dark Day, Countryside 17, 37*), the Spirit of Earth. But for us the audience there is a much more obvious explanation for the mysterious hints from the spirit world that prompt Faust's different translations (*1225, 1228, 1235*): he is, after all, closeted with the Devil, even if in the form of a poodle. In rejecting 'the word' Faust is not only, in theory and in practice, rejecting the hold of verbal tradition on his mind: he is also rejecting a particular tradition, 'the Word' that is Christ. For that tradition he is substituting, though in words as similar as possible to the old, a new, post-Christian understanding of human nature. The paradox that Faust still pretends to be translating the Gospel of the Christ whom he rejects is the paradox of all the 'reinterpretations' of Christianity in which nineteenth- and twentieth-century German theology and philosophy are so rich, and it is here expressed in the irony that Faust's mistranslation is deliberate and conscious (*1227*). His aim, like that of much modern biblical, and literary, criticism, is not the interpretation of an authoritative original but the assertion of his own freedom. Faust's act of defining himself *against* the spirit of the New Testament, which parallels other more explicit rejections or inversions of Christianity in earlier tellings of his story, is the signal for his future interlocutor, the 'spirit [he] can grasp', to declare himself too.

Lines 1238–1326 (P72–4, E40–3)

That Mephistopheles is essentially a Christian devil is shown both by the metamorphoses of the strangely swelling beast, reminiscent of the transformations of Satan in *Paradise Lost*, and by Faust's exorcisms, for he responds not to the conjuration of the four natural elements (*1271–91*), but to the crucifix (*1300*) (a motif already present in the suppressed *Urfaust* scene, *High Road*). Mephistopheles' entrance line (*1322*), however, has a comic tone which will be characteristic of his entire future role − deflating the pretensions of Faust's noisy eloquence − which makes it impossible to take the preceding pantomime seriously. Faust himself laughs (*1324*). Goethe is here treating his material with deliberate artificiality and allusiveness, caricaturing it in fact: the space behind the stove from which Mephistopheles emerges (*1188*, *1310*, after *1320*) is known in German as 'Hell' (*die Hölle*), and the offer of an unenticing or wearisomely familiar attraction − such as the traditional hocus-pocus of a Faust play − is dismissed with the idiomatic phrase, 'that won't draw the dog from behind the stove' ('das lockt keinen Hund hinterm Ofen hervor'). (Conversely, line *1323* has itself subsequently become proverbial.)

Lines 1327–1529 (P74–81, E43–50)

Faust himself seems familiar to the point of boredom with the ways of devils, their names (*1332*), and their habit of entering rooms through chimneys (*1392*), and displays a frigid lack of interest in whether Mephistopheles stays or goes

(*1388–90*). He mentions 'a pact' as if it were a well-known item of commerce between men and devils (*1414–15*), requiring no further explication. Mephistopheles, who is dressed more or less as the legend requires of him at his first appearance, assures Faust that he will be given all that tradition promises (*1416–17*) – a remark that could equally be addressed by Goethe to his audience – but insists, without giving a reason, that an agreement must wait until their next meeting. Goethe's audience is presumed to know that Faust 'always' has two conversations with Mephistopheles before he makes his pact. None the less, by the end of the present scene Faust has already received all the pleasures for which traditionally he bartered his soul; and unlike the authors of the Faust Books Goethe does not find it necessary to send his hero to Hell in order to prove their insubstantiality. A hangover is sufficient.

This high degree of literary self-consciousness is essential to the function of the whole scene. We are being shown that the life of a Faust who has translated the central notions of traditional Christianity into his own modern idiom cannot be narrated in a simple retelling of the traditional legend. The Faust story has to be translated too. We are being prepared for the highly paradoxical scene which is to come, in which a post-Christian man will make an agreement with a Christian Devil. For, Goethe's poem is asking us at this point, what form could we *seriously* expect such an agreement to take? It cannot be an agreement in accordance with the 'law[s] of spirits and ghosts' (*1410*), which work by chalk lines and pentagrams, whose artificiality is manifestly ludicrous and which have no further significant role in the play. A Faust story based on that conception of God, man and the Devil could compel neither ethical nor dramatic attention. A second conversation between Faust and Mephistopheles is necessary – one which will start from quite different premises.

Already, however, the revolutionary translation of St John, which defines Faust's modernity, is a sign of his tragic flaw, and Mephistopheles alludes to it immediately (*1327–30*). The man who set out to seek the source of all life

has passed within an ace of suicide and is on the point of binding himself to the spirit of evil; but, since the passionate
energy which inspires him has been directed into a rejection
of the traditional 'words' by which moral and religious value
is expressed, he is oblivious of this decline and defenceless
against it. Mephistopheles announces his own nature and
moral function with the naive directness of a figure in a
puppet-play (*1335–6*) and with the comically ingratiating ex-
asperation of a Devil part of whose torment is to see the futili-
ty of his own malice (as in *1362–78*). Yet these plain words are
to Faust an 'enigma', and he ignores entirely Mephistopheles'
next profession of loyalty to sin and moral evil (*1345*) – the
very form in which a human spirit *can* be expected to 'grasp'
the negative component in the all-embracing Spirit of Earth.
Only a flowery cosmological myth briefly attracts Faust's
curiosity (*1342–61*). The enemy of words hears only those
words he wishes to hear (*1423*). Moreover, he claims not to
have set out to entrap Mephistopheles (*1426*), when we know
that he has consistently sought an association such as this.
Already the omens are not good.

The second *Study* scene, Goethe's modern version of Faust's
pact with the Devil, is the longest passage of sustained
abstract argument in the play. This scene may have been in
Goethe's mind when he wrote to Schiller on 18 March 1801:
'Though since this work arouses the curiosity of the
philosophers I clearly have to watch my step.' It stands out
from practically all other scenes in the play in not being built
round some strong, simple visual impression or series of
impressions: there is only Mephistopheles' brilliant clothing,
symbolising as he says the 'colourful new life' (*1121*) to which
he intends to introduce Faust (*1540–3, 2072*), and the document which Faust signs in his blood. Otherwise this scene, in
which Faust's 'abstruse speculations' reach their peak, is a
matter entirely of 'words'.

Lines 1530–1634 (P82–5, E51–4)

Faust reacts to Mephistopheles' sprightly proposal with his

most violent and general expression of despair. The ambition
to share the life of the entire universe has been eclipsed by the
rejection that ambition implies of all particular and individual
experience, which can only seem inadequate to so endless an
appetite. Faust rejects the later Goethe's morality of 'renunciation' (*1549*) without any compensating reference to a desire
to contemplate the deep things of the world (*384*) or to grasp
the breasts of life (*456*). Existence is now pure deprivation
that cannot in principle fulfil a single one of his wishes (*1557*)
There is an absolute disjunction between the desires of which
he feels himself composed, and which deserve to be called
divine, and the world which is not himself but in which those
desires need to be realised (*1566–9*). Faust is no more able to
overcome this abstract, indeed philosophical, opposition of
inner and outer worlds than when he was on the brink of
suicide, and the immediate prelude to the wager is a
recapitulation of the suicide theme and its associated
incidents from the scene *Night* (*1570–86*).

Despite his susceptibility to the memory of childish
religion, Faust now unambiguously rejects the entire intellectual and moral content of religion, the culture and the value
it imposes. He curses not only the deceitful stories of religion
but the whole of what philosophers call sensuous appearance
(*1593*), everything that is not his inmost soul full of it
insatiable longings; and his curse culminates in the rejection
of the three supreme, or theological, Christian virtues: love
both of God and of man, hope and faith, together with the
attitude of patient suffering they entail (*1604–6*). But in the
very moment in which Faust expresses total nihilism and
denies value to anything whatever outside himself, an invisible chorus of spirits sings of the possibility, none the less, of
a new life (*1622*). Faust is a demi-god, or titan, they sing
whose curse has destroyed the self-assured cosmos (*1609*) of
a past order; but he is, because he is semi-divine, capable of
establishing a new order, reconstructing the world 'in his
bosom' (*1621* cp. *1566*). Faust is here shown to share in the
foremost intellectual developments of Goethe's time. Like
Kant, the founding father of German Idealism, know

colloquially as 'the all-pulveriser', Faust has denied that any limited thing in the material, external, world has any value in itself. But life can be made worth living once more if, like Kant and the post-Kantian Idealists Fichte and Schelling, Faust will seek the value of things and even the world-order, not in things themselves but in his own self, 'in his bosom'. Suddenly the impotence of the god within (*1566*), shut off completely from the outside world, will be transformed into omnipotence, for suddenly all things will have value and purpose only in so far as they are subject to the rulings of that interior god. That this message is communicated to Faust by spirits of uncertain origin, but whom Mephistopheles, even if mendaciously, claims to be his servants (*1627–8*), indicates that the extreme subjectivity of Idealism, though it is not necessarily diabolical, is potentially deeply corrupting. Faust will in the rest of the play experience what he wants to experience, but precisely and only that. With two exceptions, represented by Gretchen and Helen, Faust's future life, lived by the magical power of his own subjectivity, will bring to him only experience already marked by the dead hand of his own desire. We already know from the previous scene how essentially illusory are the satisfactions Mephistopheles promises (*1631–4*). But by the very choice that opens him to those illusions Faust blinds himself to the objective reality of the moral evil that, under their cover, is endeavouring, with increasing success, to insinuate itself into his life.

Lines 1635–1711 (P85–8, E54–6)

Mephistopheles initially offers himself three times as Faust's servant on the traditional terms (*1642, 1656, 1672*), each time in vain. Faust will have to bind himself on his own initiative and in terms that he as a modern man can understand. There is nothing he can undertake to do for Mephistopheles, since he does not believe in an after-life (*1660–70*). Equally, there is nothing the Devil can offer him (*1675*), since he does not believe that anything external to himself, being of its nature limited, has any value. Value attaches only to the 'sublime striving' (*1676*) of a human soul, infinite in its capacities and ambitions. A finite real good in the world would be as paradoxical a notion as a fruit that rotted before it was ripe or trees that grew fresh leaves every day – is that the sort of thing Mephistopheles is proposing to furnish (*1678–87*)? Mephistopheles shows how difficult indeed it will be for these two to agree on anything by crassly missing Faust's rhetorical point (or by giving it the only realistic sense it has): yes, he can provide such curios, he says, as if Faust would in fact think that with them he had been given anything worth while.

That Faust's ambition for the infinite (*1815*), because it is something that cannot be put into words, is unreal, is shown by an ambiguity, of which he is unaware, in the list of what he asks for. He *intends* a list of paradoxes, as lines *1686–7* show, but *utters* a list of all-too-familiar banalities: food that does not state, money that runs away. Mephistopheles (see *1860–5*) will be only too pleased to give Faust what his words ask here and later (*1756–8, 1766–7*), for they seem to be asking for the world in the state in which the Devil sees it and to which he tries to reduce it: a pointless and worthless alternation of frustration and satiety ending in nothingness. What the Devil ignores, because Faust can never put it into words, is the infinite something else for the sake of which Faust expresses his negation of all that is. Unreal – or, as Goethe's contemporaries would have said, 'ideal' – though that something is, the ambition for it may none the less in the end be a condition of Faust's redemption (*11936–7*).

Mephistopheles now reiterates the conventional wisdom of the former age, which believed that there were good things in life, some heavenly, some earthly, and which in Mephistopheles' experience was usually prepared to settle for the earthly (*1690–1*): Faust too, despite what he says, will, Mephistopheles believes, make his compromises like the rest of us, and accept the enjoyments to be had from things of limited worth. To this challenge to his most fundamental sincerity Faust responds with a challenge of his own. Let Mephistopheles show him what he will (*1692, 1694*), it will

have no value. Nothing he will do, or will by Mephistopheles
be enabled to do, will make him go back on his curse. If he
were to go back on it he would only have been deceived by
the Devil (*1694, 1696*) and would not be worthy of life anyway.

Mephistopheles accepts the challenge with a single word
and Faust then reformulates the agreement in less dramatic
and more metaphysical terms. Influenced perhaps by
Schiller's discussion of human identity in the eleventh of his
Letters on the Aesthetic Education of Man (1795) and by the
distinction made there between the circumstances of our tran-
sient condition (*Zustand*) and our abiding identity (*Person*),
Goethe makes his Faust assert that no single passing moment
in life can be weighed up against his own self and be found
to be anything other than valueless in comparison. If he were
ever to regard one of his passing conditions as more valuable
than his underlying identity, he would effectively have
annihilated himself. His life is to be a ceaseless onward rush
through moments: if it stops once it has denied itself in principle and stopped for ever. If ever Faust says to the passing
moment, 'Linger on, you are so lovely', time for him will be
over, his self-determination will have ceased, and
Mephistopheles, or anyone else, can do with him what he will
(*1699–1706*). In so far as Faust's earlier acts of hubris − his
gesture toward suicide and his curse on life − assert his own
autonomy and the nullity of the world, they now require him
not to die but to live a life as energetically varied as possible,
and so submit his hubris (*1709*) to the most stringent test conceivable. His right to his curse, and to life after his curse, is
to be bought at the highest price imaginable (cp. J. P. Stern,
'The Dear Purchase', *German Quarterly* 41(1968) 317–37),
the price of submitting his inner self to endless valueless
experience, and if he is proved wrong he is prepared to give
up that inner self in death, for if he is wrong that inner self
is a slave to external forces and not worth having anyway
(*1710–11*). Faust has thus discovered a way of living for post-
Christian man, man after the curse, a way which positively
requires the very fullness and variety of experience for which
he yearned, and requires also that he be permanently passing

on from one momentary experience to the next, transported
as by his own magic cloak.

Lines 1712–1867 (P88–93, E56–61)

For all its appearance of being a wager, Faust's agreement
with Mephistopheles is at bottom a compact with diabolical
forces, and his apparently generous and energetic engagement
in life is tragically flawed. He proposes to experience all
human life through the agency of a destructive power:
experience will for him be synonymous with the denial of
value to that which is experienced. Life will be worth living,
though at the price of not being worth anything more than
that (cp. *1775*). In that sense Faust has deliberately let the
Devil into his life, the power of destruction in the form of
humanly comprehensible evil (*1344*), and he has allowed
Mephistopheles to take over part of his identity. This is
precisely what Mephistopheles has long desired, and for his
own reasons, which leave him with little interest in either the
form or the substance of Faust's wager, both proceeding
from presuppositions which Mephistopheles cannot share.
Mephistopheles has seen the wager, like all Faust's self-
assertion, as so much *Rednerei*, garrulous exaggeration
(*1734*). Of course, if Faust wishes to give himself up to the
Devil by uttering a verbal formula whose significance is more
or less opaque to Mephistopheles, Mephistopheles will not
object. He is willing to act as Faust's agent in procuring him
ever new experiences, but he promises himself success not
from the terms of the modernising wager but from his own
old-fashioned diabolical scheming. He welcomes Faust's new
openness to the world and the flesh (*1750–1*), but is troubled
that the paradoxical excessiveness of Faust's desires may
make him too fastidious towards the simple, well-tried vices
the Devil has to offer (*1764*, *1786*, *1828–33*). Once the long
dialogue is over he tells us in a monologue that, provided he
has control over Faust's desires and their satisfaction, he will
secure Faust's damnation – to which, Faust has told us, he
is indifferent (*1669–70*) – quite independently of any agree-

ment (*1853–5*) (*unbedingt = ohne Bedingung* = 'regardless
of our conditional agreement'; not quite 'without a saving
clause' (P), and certainly not 'beyond recall' (E)). Faust will
be ruined, not by the contract into which he has just entered,
but by the temptations and trials into which the Devil will lead
him during the time of their association (*1866–7*).

In his negotiations with Faust, Mephistopheles has achieved
his original minimal objective: to be Faust's permanent companion and servant (*1642–8*), transforming his desires into
reality, the spirit of lies (*1854*) establishing the bridge Faust
sought between the inner and the outer worlds (*1567, 1569*).
The specifically modern features of the agreement Faust has
taken so long to formulate pass him by. His attempts to
entrap Faust in accordance with the terms of the wager are
half-hearted, and he refers to it again only once, in lines
3256–7. (As these lines were first published in 1790, Faust's
first formulation of the wager (*1692–3*), to which they allude,
must already have been in existence.) Moreover, he asks Faust
for a written document, as if this Faust were not different
from the hero of the Faust-Book or of the puppet-play. Faust
sees this blunder as further evidence of the literal-mindedness
(*1716*) that could not understand his paradoxical imagery,
and of the impossibility of their ever thinking alike. How can
a piece of parchment bind him more firmly than his solemn
word? How can a word bind him, once it is seen as something
different from his own inmost self? Faust's refusal to give
value to things means, ultimately, that no pact is even possible in the traditional sense, since no obligation can be
imposed on Faust by an external authority, whether the
authority of a piece of paper, or that of the law whose sanc-
tions give weight to the piece of paper, unless Faust also
imposes that obligation on himself by his own free choice –
in which case the external authority is of course superfluous.
Faust is interested only in living by the spirit of the wager, not
in its letter, and Mephistopheles promises himself success, not
in the first instance from the letter of his agreement with Faust,
but from the opportunity it gives to tempt and corrupt him.
Neither party is thus, strictly speaking, interested in an agree-

ment which is often said to be at the heart of the play. Goethe not only gives us two different versions of the wager in spoken form, but also refrains from telling us which words precisely are written on the document to which Faust appends his signature in blood. There could not be a clearer warning that quibbling over the terms of a contract is not what his play is about.

But of course this scene does show us what the play is about, even though what it shows is a tension of which both the parties involved are unaware. The most important source of tension in the play is the question which we as readers now ask ourselves: which of the protagonists will be proved right by the event – Faust, with his 'sublime striving' (*1676*), which to Mephistopheles is mere exaggeration and verbiage (*1740–1815*), or Mephistopheles, with his hidden intention of moral corruption, visible to us but concealed from Faust by his own choice? Can the Faustian, that is, the consciously modern, post-Christian life be led in total self-consistency without so compromising itself morally that only the traditional Christian categories of sin and atonement are adequate to describe it? Can the attempt to lead, within the confines of ordinary humanity, the life beyond good and evil lived by the Spirit of Earth result in anything more grand than simple, limited, human, wrongdoing? The real wager, ultimately, is Goethe's wager with his own poetic powers: can he convince his readers that, in his representation of his own modern age, he has not made things too easy for Faust, if Faust succeeds, or that he has not succumbed to too easy a despair if Faust's grand venture fails? In his working out of the central tension in *Faust* we shall find much that is surprising or bizarre, but nothing that is facile.

As in the scene *Night*, in which the discussion with Wagner followed on the emotionally exhausting confrontation with the Spirit of Earth, so now the climax that is the 'wager' – as we may for convenience call that complex agreement – is followed by a change of tonality. After the wager Faust i

emotionally drained, his language becomes more frenetic and
then dries up, and Mephistopheles clearly asserts his control
(see P. Requadt, *Goethes 'Faust I'. Leitmotivik und
Architektur* (Munich, 1972), pp. 171–93). In the three follow-
ing, predominantly comic, scenes, the dramatic tension is
relaxed: the scene between Mephistopheles and the student,
Auerbach's Cellar in Leipzig, and *Witch's Kitchen*. The narrative sequence, hitherto fairly continuous, now starts to
fragment, in preparation for the episodic structure of the
Gretchen story. But though their relation to each other in
time is obscure, these three scenes are linked by a common
concern with Faust's identity after the wager and the extent
to which Mephistopheles has usurped Faust's personality, or
established his power over it.

Lines 1868–2050 (P93–9, E61–8)

The light-hearted satire, in the scene with the Student, one of
the oldest in the play, fills out the picture of the university
world, the starting-point which Faust is leaving behind. Like
Outside the Gates it reminds us that, whatever Faust may
think, his life has an objective social and historical
background – from which eventually Gretchen will emerge.
Mephistopheles throughout this scene impersonates Faust,
wearing his academic robes: after the wager even the role in
which Faust has in the past had his firmest footing in social
existence is now filled with cynical negativity – the Devil's
takeover is already well advanced. Furthermore, the scene
extensively complements Mephistopheles' self-characterisation
in his monologue (*1851–67*): he is, in his intentions, a traditional Christian devil, seeking to lead into fleshly temptation
(*2010*) the ingenuous young student who himself has Faustian
traits (*1899–1901*), and giving as his autograph the words of
the serpent in the Book of Genesis (*2048*).

Lines 2051–72 (P99, E68–9)

In the little epilogue, or transition scene, at the end of

Study II we see the two travellers, as they have now become with Faust's definitive rejection of his former life, stepping on to the magic cloak for which Faust once so eloquently expressed his longing. Now that his ambition for new life has been fulfilled (*2072* cp. *1121*) he cuts a sorry figure, expressing his fear that he is too old and unused to the world to be able to enjoy it, no longer knowing where he wants to go (contrast *1087*, *1123*) and having to ask Mephistopheles, on whom he is now apparently dependent, for suggestions (*2051*). Mephistopheles seems initially to have two ideas in mind – the pleasures of drink and of love, both roundly cursed by Faust before the wager (*1603–4*). These together will constitute a visitation of the 'microcosm', the little world of the human body (see H. Jantz, *The Form of Faust* (Baltimore and London, 1978), pp. 107–13), before Faust proceeds to the greater world – one of the few hints in *Part One* that beyond it lies *Part Two* with its historical world of public, political and economic action (*2052*).

Lines 2073–336 (P100–10, E69–82)

Auerbach's Cellar in Leipzig, another of the oldest scenes in the play, dramatises a legend current in Leipzig when Goethe was a student there, that Dr Faust had visited this famous tavern and flown out of it on a wine-barrel. In *Urfaust* it plainly has the function of standing for numerous scenes in traditional Faust plays in which Faust uses his magical powers to play practical jokes and lead a merry life before his time runs out. In *Part One* that function is singularly modified. Far from having a merry time, Faust is here as miserable as he had predicted (*2055–60*), saying nothing whatever after his initial greeting (*2183*) until he utters the classic epitaph on an evening's fiasco (*2296*). All the conjuring and jocularity is left to Mephistopheles, since for the Faust of *Part One* these pleasures have no appeal. If this is all Mephistopheles has to offer, Faust's wager is easily won: he will have no difficulty in denying value to *this* experience. If Faust is to be restricted to the experiences traditionally

provided in the old plays, he will never emerge from the
suicidal depression of the scenes *Night* and *Study I* and *II*.
Meanwhile, Mephistopheles' devilish nature is sinisterly rein-
forced (*2300–1, 2321*).

Lines 2337–604 (P110–20, E83–93)

Witch's Kitchen, with its artificial and tedious stage business
and Faust's monotonous exclamations of disgust, is the least
satisfactory scene in *Part One*. Maybe this is because it was
composed in Italy, at a time when Goethe was out of sympathy with the world of *Urfaust*. (*Urfaust* contains only one
passing reference to witches, whom Goethe seems in later life
to have regarded as an essential component of the Faust
legend.) None the less *Witch's Kitchen* is a turning-point in
the action of the play, a conclusion to what has gone before
which also initiates a completely new phase in the story.
Superficially, the permanent rejuvenation of Faust by thirty
years (*2342*), which the witch's potion accomplishes, is essential if he is to experience all that life has to offer and if he is
to be relaunched after the false start of *Auerbach's Cellar*.
More profoundly, the scene makes explicit the theme of sexuality, hitherto only implied by Faust's rhetorical imagery.
Two distinct and opposed attitudes to love are presented from
the start. For Mephistopheles, love is simply a matter of sexuality, purely animal and preferably perverse. Here, as later,
he is shown to have an erotic relation with the witches who
serve him, being recognised by an obscene gesture (*2513*)
rather than any more traditional accoutrement of the Devil
(*2490–1*), making an obscene allusion to the resurgence of
Faust's virility after he drinks the potion (*2598*), and telling
him that any woman will be as good as any other for the
satisfaction of the desire now infused into his body (*2603–4*).
Faust by contrast is attracted even before he takes the drink
to an ideal, unapproachable (*2433–5*) vision of female beauty
provided by the witch's magic mirror (*2429–40*). Even before
Mephistopheles has awakened his physical lust he wants to
leave all the witch's paraphernalia to pursue this ideal

(*2461–2*), which, after the potion, he still finds more attractive than Mephistopheles' promises of physical enjoyment (*2599–602*). Even though this vision of the ideal far transcends the Devil's comprehension, Faust, after the wager, can experience it only by magical means, and it is here that the scene's deepest significance lies.

For Faust has bound himself to the Devil (*2504–5*), to the prince of this world, crowned with a broken crown (*2448–9*), who regards his kingdom as worthless, a hollow, easily fractured bauble (*2402–15*), a dirty joke that occasions only heartless, inhuman laughter. In draining the potion, Faust accepts the Mephistophelean nature into his innermost being (*2594–5*), the flames that lap around the cup recall the hellish liquor of *Auerbach's Cellar*, and the cup itself recalls the poison draught he did not drink on Easter Sunday morning. Allowing the power of the Devil to suffuse his body and soul is the next-best substitute for suicide, the highest degree of negativity compatible with continuing in life at all, the physical representation of Faust's intimate union with the curse on life and the belief in the valuelessness of the world. That union, in the wager, is the presupposition of all Faust's subsequent experience. Just as the magic cloak will make it possible for Faust to flit from one experience to the next without restriction, connection or consequence, and by that very inconsequentiality will detach him from every normal human community, so the witch's potion will make all human experience available to Faust, but by giving him a body not susceptible to the dilapidation, ageing and alteration inseparable from any normal human experience whatever. The magical, unnatural, means, even in respect of his own body, that Faust has adopted to fulfil his ambition are contrasted with the life of a healthy, untroubled peasant who tills the soil and lives out his eighty years in acceptance of his circumscribed lot (*2353–61*). If Faust is not willing to accept the restrictions of a position in the social, religious, historical or even natural order, in the 'constricted life' (*2364*), he must have recourse to magic (*2365*). Far from being the life of a typical or supreme human being, Faust's is the tragic and self distorting life of a modern man who takes the non-natural, subjective, magical path. Another path is possible, 'but it is written in another book, and makes strange reading' (*2349–50*) – perhaps, for example, it is written in Goethe's novel *Wilhelm Meister's Years of Wandering* of which the sub-title is *Tales of Renunciation*. In Faust's own book that path is taken by Gretchen, Faust's principal dramatic antagonist, to whose story *Witch's Kitchen* is the introduction. For the story of Faust and Gretchen tells of the collision between the modern, unrestricted, emancipated human being and the representative of the traditional, limited, moral order in its most attractive and fulfilling form, an order which Faust has none the less violently put behind him.

Chapter 4

Love

(Street – Evening – Promenade – The Neighbour's House – Street – Garden – A Summerhouse)

Faust is filled with desire for a young town-girl, Margarete ('Gretchen' for short). Mephistopheles, at first unwilling to assist, provides Faust with access to Gretchen's room and gifts of jewellery for her. He arranges a rendezvous in the garden of a neighbour, Mistress Martha, provided Faust is prepared to testify falsely to the death of Martha's husband. Mephistopheles mocks Faust's squeamish reluctance to do so and predicts that Faust will soon practise worse deceit on Gretchen. In the garden Gretchen tells of her simple home life with her widowed mother, and of her infant sister, now dead, whom she brought up as if her own child. Faust passionately declares a love which he says must last for ever. Gretchen runs off to a summerhouse where she declares her own love and the two exchange kisses. Mephistopheles interrupts this high point of Faust's experience, and Faust leaves.

In *Urfaust* the story of Faust and Gretchen is told in fifteen short scenes which form a single dramatic crescendo of almost unbearable emotional intensity. In *Part One* this development is interrupted, and its effect moderated, by two retarding scenes, *Forest, Cavern* and *Walpurgis Night*, with the associated *Walpurgis Night's Dream*. The love story is now being told less as a drama in its own right than as a component in the picture of Faust's ambition and its consequences. In *Part One*, too, the scene *Witch's Kitchen* casts a strange light over everything that follows. When in 1829 Goethe read through *Part One* with the actors who were putting on the play's first full performance in Weimar, he made a point of adopting a falsetto voice for Faust in all the scenes after the rejuvenating potion has been drunk. That point was well taken by Gustaf Gründgens in his film version of the play: before *Witch's Kitchen* Faust is a desperate but honest middle-aged man; after it he is a grotesquely titivated spiv. It is Gretchen's merit to see through the cosmetic surface to the human being wilfully hidden away within. She thus reveals that there are more things in heaven and earth than were dreamt of in the philosophy that led Faust to make his compact with the Devil.

Lines 2605–77 (P121–3, E94–6)

The first impression left by the first scene entitled *Street* might well be that Mephistopheles' prediction of the effects of the witch's potion is proving correct. Faust's feeling for Gretchen, if that is what it can be called, is simply an animal desire to sleep with her this very night (*2637*). Yet even in his first reactions to her brisk rejection of his advances there is an appreciation, however patronising, of her independent personality (*2609–18*). Faust's flattering courtesies (Fräulein (*2605*) was a term of address for a noblewoman; cp. *2906*) would put her in a higher class than she belongs to, but the very self-confidence of her dismissive reply indicates a knowledge of her own worth and perhaps even a pleasure in its being noticed. She is no non-entity. Mephistopheles immediately reacts to keep Faust away from her (*2621–6*): he scents danger in this innocent figure, so close to the bosom of the Church, who will more than once be compared to an angel of heaven (*2708, 2712, 3124*) and who will indeed in the distant future serve precisely that function, to Mephistopheles' permanent discomfiture. That he recognises her innocence does not prevent him from immediately laying plans for her seduction and ruin. He sees in her an alien power (*2626*) which threatens his own exclusive hold over Faust. Once he realises that Faust's attraction to her is strong, and emphatically carnal (*2627*), his appearance of reluctance, and creation of delays, is only a pretence designed to tantalise Faust and increase his appetite. Mephistopheles' ability to spy on Gretchen's doings (*2623*) and predict her movements (*2668*) is unsettling, even menacing.

Lines 2678–804 (P123–8, E97–101)

Short though the scenes of the Gretchen story are, they are often subdivided into even shorter episodes. In *Street* a monologue of Faust's separates two dialogues, with Gretchen and Mephistopheles, respectively. In *Evening* there are at least five units – a monologue of Gretchen's, two dialogues between Faust and Mephistopheles, separated by a long monologue of Faust's, and into Gretchen's final monologue is inserted the singing of a ballad. The action moves rapidly but leaves an impression of fullness, both through its variety and through its emotional reflection in monologues and songs, whose individuality is enhanced by their association with a physical action (Gretchen's combing her hair), or an object (the simple furniture of her room), or something as subtle as a scent or even just a time of day. In these scenes Goethe's poetic art is at its most condensed and pictorial. By the end of *Evening* we already have a strong impression of Gretchen's character, and Faust's career has evidently taken a new and unexpected turn.

Gretchen, in these early scenes, is not characterised simply by innocence, or goodness, or the orderly and industrious selflessness of her life, or even her latent, normal sensuality. Rather we see in her a harmony, both natural and willed, of everything that she is with the social and religious limitations of her world. She is the perfect manifestation of the possibility of human happiness and goodness within 'the constricted life' (*2364*) which Faust believed was incompatible with happiness and to which, as to all limited things, he refused the name of good. When Gretchen, combing her hair, wonders who the noble and attractive stranger might be who has taken such liberties with the conventions she acknowledges, this is not a sign of some conflict between her desires and the

principles in which she has been brought up. She is not innocent, if that means ignorant of the ways of the world, but
there can be no conflict between her natural desires, of which
she is fully aware, and her goodness, because to Gretchen
moral goodness itself is perfectly natural. When she discovers
the chest of jewels she says with equal naturalness and in
adjacent lines:

> Wie sollte mir die Kette stehn?   (*2794*)

(I wonder how the chain would suit me?)

and

> Wem mag die Herrlichkeit gehören?   (*2795*)

(Who can this finery belong to?)

She quite unfearingly acknowledges the appeal the jewellery
has for her, but it does not even cross her mind to misap-
propriate it (cp. *2909*). She wishes the jewels were hers but she
accepts unquestioningly the sadness that they are not
(*2802–4*). In singing the ballad 'There was a king in Thule' she
allows herself to dwell on what would be the fulfilment of her
desires, and it is simply the pefection of what is possible
within the world she knows – a completely happy, wholly
faithful and physically fortunate love that lasts into and
beyond death, though whether inside or outside marriage is
left significantly unclear.

Faust is transformed (*2720*) by his entry into Gretchen's
room. He repeatedly describes it in religious terms, as a 'holy
place' (*2688*) or a 'heaven' (*2708*), feels in it the presence not
of her body but of her 'spirit' (*2702*), and admits that his
physical desires have drained away (*2722* cp. *2647*). Most
importantly, this little world, so limited in physical terms, in
which simple objects such as a chair or a tablecloth or the
sand on the floor have a spiritual significance (*2695–701*,
2705–6), is a place in which human fulfilment and happiness
is possible and indeed achieved:

> In dieser Armut welche Fülle!
> In diesem Kerker welche Seligkeit!   (*2693–4*)

(In this poverty, what abundance! In this prison, what bliss!)

Faust is on the point of falling in love with the 'constricted life', which he has just violently rejected in *Witch's Kitchen*. Aware, perhaps, of the possible consequences for this narrow world of his intrusion into it, Faust resolves to leave and not return (*2750*).

Mephistopheles is clearly acting as diabolical tempter when he distracts Faust from this resolution by producing the casket of jewels previously demanded by Faust (*2731*), and then himself shuts the casket away in Gretchen's cupboard. In order to consent to the scheme Faust has to do nothing except leave the room (*2745, 2752*). Faust's hesitation (*2738*) indicates that the moral responsibility for continuing with the conspiracy none the less remains with him. The Devil does everything to make them easy for him but these actions are his own.

The deep hostility between Gretchen and Mephistopheles is evident from the moment of Mephistopheles' entry into this place of purity and order. He sniffs around it like the dog he once was (before *2686*), and does his best to pollute it by recalling to Faust's mind the disarray in which many other girls live. What to Faust is a 'magic scent' (*2721*) in an atmosphere which breathes calm and content (*2691–2*) Mephistopheles has already referred to contemptuously as Gretchen's 'aura' (*Dunstkreis, 2671*), and Gretchen senses the contamination when she returns to her room and finds it stuffy and oppressive, and opens the window. Though as far as she knows her fear is groundless, she feels something evil and frightening in the air (*2753–8*).

Lines 2805–64 (P128–30, E101–3)

In the scene *Promenade* a comic tone enters with Mephistopheles' mocking allusions to his diabolical status (*2805–6, 2809–10*), with his satirical pictures of the avaricious and hypocritical priest and of Gretchen's fearsomely pious mother, who have combined to defeat the ploy with the jewel-

casket, and with his sarcastic adoption of the role of over-
worked and underpaid servant of a demanding master (*2856,
2861*). But he retains his sinister ability to spy on the secret
thoughts and emotions of other characters (*2816, 2849–52*),
which he reports in such a way as to further his designs on
Faust (*2827–30, 2852*), while Faust's command to produce a
second casket is abrupt and almost angry, as if it troubled his
conscience.

Lines 2865–3024 (P130–6, E104–11)

The comedy now develops into a more elaborate digression.
Mephistopheles, in the *The Neighbour's House*, remains in
appearance the witty, ironical and worldly wise humorist, and
we can enjoy his ingenious practical joking with Mistress
Martha because we recognise the entirely conventional nature
of her sorrow for her supposedly dead husband (*2872*). But
there is no mistaking the underlying ruthlessness with which
he is deviously pursuing the aim of an assignation between
Faust and Gretchen and which accords well with his pose as
a travelling man of quality. That hardness contrasts sharply
with Gretchen's spontaneous sympathy with Martha on the
report of her huband's death (*2919*), with her intuitive
understanding of the anguish of love bereaved (*2921–2*), with
the religious sentiment which makes it natural for her to pray
for the dead (*2942*), and with the Catholic German ambience
in which repeated exclamations of 'Ach, Gott!' have not
entirely lost an aura of piety (*2895, 2908*). Gretchen
instinctively recognises that there is something uncanny about
the presents of jewels (*2894*), even though, within the limits
of honesty (*2909*), she finds their attraction hard to resist.
The seriousness and courageousness with which she turns
aside Mephistopheles' suggestion that she should take a
lover is the very voice of what Hegel would call 'ethical
substance':

Das ist des Landes nicht der Brauch.   (*2949* cp. *3007*)

(That is not the custom in these parts.)

This polite appeal to local convention is simultaneously a statement of absolute moral principle: the divinity for which Faust vainly yearns is here found in the very limitations of the constricted life. Mephistopheles' acknowledgement of her goodness and innocence (*3007*) only sets off the coldness of his deliberate plan to use her for further corrupting Faust and for indulging his own pleasure in torture and destruction. But this negativity of Mephistopheles is the image and the contracted instrument of Faust's curse on life − and so on the life of Gretchen which is gradually being revealed to him and us.

Lines 3025–72 (P136–8, E111–13)

While the scenes in which Gretchen appears are all located in rooms − places of rest, defined and to some extent rendered secure by society and civilisation − the alternating scenes with Faust are in open, indefinite, characterless places not of rest, but of passage. The second *Street* scene shows Mephistopheles, delighted to have found in Martha a woman whose view of sexual relations is similar to his own (*3029–30*), isolating Faust still further from the human community by committing him to his first deliberate lie (*3038*). In the truculence of Faust's response to this suggestion (*3039*) and to Mephistopheles' prediction that he is anyway about to forswear himself to Gretchen (*3053*), and in the wildness of argument through which he allows himself to be persuaded to do what is wrong (*3050, 3067–72*), there is perhaps a dawning awareness of the dilemma into which he is being forced by his disastrous wager. He has to acknowledge an element of truth in what Mephistopheles says: what he now feels for Gretchen cannot be put into words, and any attempt to do so will be a kind of deception. But Faust also asserts emphatically that there is something of eternal value in his feeling, to which Mephistopheles' cynicism does not begin to do justice.

Lines 3073–162 (P138–42, E114–18)

It is strange to see Faust out of his depth. In the scene

Garden the counterpointing of conversations between the two couples, Faust and Gretchen, Martha and Mephistopheles, might lead us to expect simply an alternation of comic and serious moments. But, although Mephistopheles' suggestive banter with Martha continues his earlier play on her hopes of catching a better husband, the dialogue between Faust and Gretchen is devoted to more than a gradual declaration of mutual love. There is an ironical element in it too, and at Faust's expense. Gretchen's long account of her maternal care for her infant sister gives a picture of her ideal of human happiness fulfilled in domesticity, as it were, in marriage. This contrast, and complement, to Mephistopheles' description of the constricted life in *Witch's Kitchen* is particularly heartrending if we reflect that Gretchen is instead destined to become an infanticide. Faust, who will bring about that destruction of an ideal which, along with everything else, he has wagered will be inadequate to the demands of his own subjectivity, is himself inadequate to respond. He has little to say and that little is platitudinous and condescending: he sees and loves the human worth that Gretchen represents, but he does not know how to talk to her (*3102–5, 3124, 3136*).

Lines 3163–204 (P142–4, E118–20)

However, the relationship changes when Faust repents of his initial importunate approach to Gretchen (*3166–8*). To come close to her he must accept the conventions outside which she could not live and still be herself. But Gretchen is not wholly a creature of her environment: despite what she knows to be accepted as right and wrong, she feels that something makes Faust dear to her (*3177–8*). What that is, and that it also transcends mere physical desire, is expressed more delicately and precisely than ever Faust manages, for all his intensely personal and wordy expressions of the inexpressible, when she infuses into a traditional game a uniquely personal meaning, as she plucks the petals of the daisy flower (*3179*). And even Faust, when he clasps Gretchen's hands and says to her the very words that Mephistopheles predicted he would say

(*3188–94* cp. *3052–4, 3055–8*), is none the less not practising a 'devilish display of lies' (*3066*). Something in Gretchen transcends the social and religious loyalties which define her existence, and it enables her to value Faust even though he lives outside those loyalties. And something in Faust escapes the all-pervading negativity which has by his own choice suffused his life, something which enables him to value Gretchen even though her existence is defined by those loyalties from which he has, emphatically, detached himself. Gretchen tells Faust that the name of that something is love (*3184*). Faust, as always, cannot remain satisfied with a name (*3186*, cp. *3061, 3063*). 'The fire that burns' him (*3064*), evoked in the unrhymed free verse reserved for the play's emotional peaks, is instead explicitly linked with the terms of the wager on which his life hangs (*3188–94*). Faust in fact comes within a hair's breadth of losing the wager both in letter and in spirit. He can give, even admittedly inadequate, expression to his bliss (*3191*) only by saying that it must last for ever – an end to it would be despair (*3193*), the very state from which he began (*610*). But to say that a moment is infinitely important and that what it contains must last for ever is not the same as asking that moment to linger, and the difference is not a quibble. Faust, who denied that the world contained any finite good, has found in it instead an infinite good. But this in turn means that he has come close to losing the wager at a deeper level than that of mere formulae. He who saw nothing of value in life to compare with his inner self, and even saw life as the minimal alternative to suicide, has found something so valuable that it is the very negation of suicidal despair and requires the complete surrender of self (*3191*, *sich hinzugeben ganz*). Why does Faust not in fact lose the wager at this point? First, because he chooses not to. Not that there is now a second moment of decision, supplanting the moment of the wager: *Faust* is not a psychological drama of that, Schillerian, kind. In making the wager Faust committed himself to the condition that even were he to achieve what then seemed impossible – insight and access into an eternal good – his experience of it should be limited to a single moment. The play so far has been the portrait of a man who so values his own subjectivity that he makes that choice, and the penalty for this choice is the tragedy that will now follow. Secondly, Faust has anyway not lost the wager in any terms that Mephistopheles can comprehend. The love which Faust and Gretchen have discovered is not anything in which Mephistopheles believes, and the words Faust uses to speak of it are so much more 'gabble' (*Rednerei*) of a kind with which he is familiar and which he can indeed predict. Mephistopheles thinks he knows all too well what it is that is drawing his two butterflies (*3203*) together: it is 'the way of the world' (*3204*); and perhaps he thinks that for Faust too at last the time has come 'when we like to chew a tasty morsel in peace' (*1691*). But, thirdly, though for us, the readers, the Faust who made the wager may have been proved wrong, Mephistopheles has not yet by any means been proved right.

Lines 3205–16 (P144, E120–1)

If Mistress Martha's garden is neither one of the rooms in which we have seen Gretchen nor one of the open spaces in which we have seen Faust, the *Summerhouse* is both at once: the summerhouse, the point of junction of nature and society, is frequently in eighteenth-century fiction the place in which a love affair is consummated. This scene crowns the process by which the previous six scenes have associated Faust's experience of love with both laughter and touching domestic intimacy, with hints of the flowers and the longer, but still cool, evenings of spring, with a world in which nature and desire are not boundless but tempered by society and brought down to the scale of human love in a garden. This scene, together with the opening of the next, constitutes an arcadian moment in *Part One*, corresponding to an extended arcadian episode in *Part Two*. But in this moment of culmination, the moment of Gretchen's response to Faust, in which their fates are bound together, a quiet note of discord portends the coming collision. The only other scene in *Part One* in which we see Faust and Gretchen together in a room is the last.

Two lines and a stage action express the supreme moment of Faust's life on earth, which passes away, however, as it comes into being. As Gretchen returns his kiss and makes her own declaration, addressing him for the first time with the intimate *du* (*3206*), Faust is for a fraction of time the passive recipient of the substantial good in life that originates outside his own subjectivity: he receives the revelation and the gift of love. Immediately Mephistopheles interrupts. The specification of Martha's entry (*3208*), not present in *Urfaust*, makes it plain that the timing is Mephistopheles' own. Perhaps he expects to find Faust 'deceived by enjoyment' (*1696*) but, as Faust's exasperated interjection reminds us (*3207*), Mephistopheles, who first appeared as a dog, has no understanding whatever of the *human* achievement on which he is intruding: his conception of love is purely animal. That this conception is quite inadequate to what has taken place in Faust since he first met Gretchen is shown by the contrast between Faust's present offer of his arm (*3208*) and that which opened their acquaintance (*2605–6*). Faust's interest is now not in a body but in an independent person, whose submission to restriction and authority, such as her mother (*3209*), he does not share but, for the present moment at least, respects and accepts. However, in the very promise of another meeting, and the expectation of a more intimate conversation still, we are warned that a disagreement between Faust and Gretchen has been postponed but not eliminated. Their love is now expressed but their worlds remain unreconciled. Mephistopheles, though he is only an animal, is none the less still Faust's 'good friend' (*3207*), and his companionship cannot be shrugged off by insults. Gretchen too, in her ingenuous concluding lines (*3211–16*), bears more eloquent witness than she realises to the difference between the lovers, even if she is as yet unaware of the tragic implications of their division. Yet the light shed by this little scene outshines even impending tragedy. There is now more, far more, to life and eternity than Faust – let alone Mephistopheles – ever dreamt of.

There is even, in this suddenly expanded life and eternity, room for the redemption of a man who gave himself up to the Devil so convinced was he that life and eternity were for him no more than a prison.

Chapter 5

Guilt

(*Forest, Cavern – Gretchen's Room – Martha's Garden – At the Well – Town Wall, Alley – Night (Street outside Gretchen's door) – Cathedral*)

Recognising their incompatibility, Faust withdraws from Gretchen, and finds the whole world of living Nature now opened to him. But Mephistopheles seeks Faust out, stirs up his carnal desire and tempts him to return. Despite the profound difference in their religious attitudes, Faust and Gretchen consummate their love, while Gretchen's mother is quietened by a sleeping-draught. Gretchen's apprehensions grow over the next days or weeks. Her brother Valentin is brought home by rumours of the affair but on surprising Faust and Mephistopheles at Gretchen's window is paralysed by Mephistopheles and killed by Faust, denouncing his sister as he dies. The two criminals, now outlaws, flee. A demon reproaches Gretchen with her pregnancy and with the deaths of Valentin and of her mother, killed by the sleeping-draught.

Forest, Cavern is, like *Witch's Kitchen*, both a scene of recollection and a turning-point in the action. It expands and dwells on the significance of the moment of love in *A Summerhouse* and of Faust's commitment to the terms of his wager. And it prepares for the consequence of that commitment, the collision between the worlds of Faust and Gretchen which follows almost immediately in the scene *Martha's Garden*. A dreamlike or, rather, nightmarish element enters into the play as the relatively lucid time-structure of the previous eight scenes breaks down into a succession of fearsomely vivid images of increasing anguish, standing in no explicit time-relation to one another. Finally, the sequence explodes into the living nightmare of the Walpurgis Night.

Lines 3217–50 (P145–6, E122)

Faust's withdrawal into a wilderness of forest-clad mountains is explicable dramatically as a flight (*3330–1*) from involvement with Gretchen, to protect her from the disaster he knows he threatens to bring her (*3348–60*), a motive with which we are already familiar (*2730*) and which is rendered urgent by the hints of conflict at the end of *A Summerhouse*. Poetically, the whole of *Forest, Cavern* is a reflective expansion of the implications of the previous scene: the withdrawal from Gretchen, an act of renunciation which acknowledges her independent identity, brings with it the very fulfilment the Faust who made the wager had declared impossible. But to the Faust who made the wager this renunciation is by the same token itself impossible except as a fleeting moment. By his own choice, it cannot be the permanent condition of his life.

The opening monologue, of great splendour, written probably while Goethe was in Italy, is one of the only two passages of blank iambic pentameter verse in the whole of *Faust*, the other being Faust's greeting to Helena, Gretchen's counterpart in *Part Two* (*9192–212*). The mutual declaration of love between Faust and Gretchen has forged a link to which time and distance are irrelevant, we learn, in two further solemn iambic pentameter lines later in the scene:

> Ich bin ihr nah, und wär ich noch so fern,
> Ich kann sie nie vergessen, nie verlieren.   (*3332–3*)

(I am near to her, however far away, I never can forget her, never lose her.)

Faust now utters a hymn of thanks to the Spirit of Earth, the most nearly divine power that he knows, for the gift he has received, the fulfilment, proceeding from the moment of renunciatory love with Gretchen, of all his yearnings in the scene *Night*. Since those yearnings had seemed doomed to frustration, Faust wagered that, his own subjectivity being the only source of value, nothing outside that subjectivity could ever have value for him – there was nothing the world, or at any rate the Devil, had to give (*1675*). But now Gretchen, another subjectivity, not something Faust could ever make, has become of eternal (*3193*) importance to him. Her love has come to him as a gift, and so Faust has discovered that he is not the maker of value in life, but that life itself is a gift. That truth Mephistopheles denies and, because the wager denies it too, it is a pact with the Devil. But because Mephistopheles denies that truth he is not able to see that, even if the wager is not strictly speaking lost, the premiss on which it was made, the premiss also of Faust's suicide gesture and his curse, has now been vitiated.

At the time when he wrote the wager scene, around 1800, Goethe had twice already, in major poems of surpassing depth and richness, depicted female figures as the pure and unearned gift (*dōron* in Greek) of God to man – Dora in *Alexis and Dora* (1796), Dorothea in *Hermann and Dorothea* (1797), though the most poignant and complex depiction was still to come in the heroine of *Pandora* (1807–10). Three times the word '(you) gave' (*gabst*) recurs in the opening lines of Faust's monologue (*3217*, *3220*). Throughout the speech, in contrast with everything he has said hitherto in the play, Faust assigns himself a passive role: all activity is attributed to the Spirit, his munificent teacher and guide (see the verbs in *3222–3*, *3225–6*, *3232*). Even the truths about Faust's own soul do not originate with him but reveal themselves by their own power (*3234*). In a landscape setting reminiscent of his earlier vision (*386–97*) Faust gives thanks for a stable intimacy of enjoyment (*3221*) with the living world of Nature (*414*), which has come to him not as something grasped (*455*) but something given (*3220*). The occasion of the gift is gently alluded to: Nature's breast, no longer the object of sensual desire (*456*), is as transparent to him as 'the bosom of a friend' (*3224*). Faust, the man who once confined all divinity to his own bosom (*1556*), now, thanks to the goodness of a friend, sees his brothers in everything that lives (*3226*). Even his own self-knowledge (*3232–4*) is presented as a consequence or corollary of his experience of Nature and of his recognition of his own limits (*3228–31* contrast *464–7*). Through knowledge of self he comes to a sympathy with history, the great human figures of the past with whom he can converse in the moonlight of reflective thought, thus fulfilling the dream conceived in his study (*3235–9* cp. *392–4*).

But Faust has been led to this glimpse of the ultimate generosity of the world and of our dependence upon it as a result of an agreement with blasphemous and devilish powers: even his inspiring vision of ideal beauty was dependent on the witch's arts. Although he now possesses an insight beyond anything Mephistopheles can understand, Faust is 'otherwise pretty well endevilled' (*3371*); he is so inextricably involved with Mephistopheles, that this deeper insight can for him be a matter only of a moment, for which the rest of his life must pay in a tragic descent into ruin. Mephistopheles, Faust's servant and also the agent of his corruption, is a principle of deception: his particular instrument is human self-deception (*3298*). He has already told us of his intention to let Faust confirm himself in error by heaping deceit on self-deceit (*1853–4*), and his entrapment of Faust begins in this scene even before his entry. Faust, in admitting his reliance on Mephistopheles, deceives himself with the description of his companion as another 'gift' from the Spirit of Earth (*3241–3*). The Spirit certainly foreshadowed the advent of another spirit, more partial and more limited than himself, whom Faust would be 'able to grasp', but Mephistopheles entered Faust's life at Faust's own request. It is by Faust's deliberate decision, and as an expression of his inmost being, that he is bound to a negativity that can make a worthless nothing of the gift of living Nature (*3246*), reduce the miracle of love to animal lust (*3247–8*), and nullify the renunciation by which Faust in withdrawing from Gretchen acknowledges her distance from him, her independence, and so her capacity to give him love in the first place. The headlong rush from one momentary state to the next, each negating the last (*3249–50*), is not the work of an alien tempter but is his own choice.

Lines 3251–373 (P146–50, E123–6)

Mephistopheles of course understands neither the love between Gretchen and Faust nor the 'lifegiving power' (*3278*)
that Faust finds in his retreat into Nature. If he did understand them, and the profound link between them as aspects
of the substantial good that Faust has after all found in life,
Mephistopheles would certainly, in his hatred of that good
(*3280–1*), take more seriously than he does (*3258*) Faust's
apparent reluctance to keep the terms of the wager and move
on to 'something new' (*3254*). In his own fashion
Mephistopheles does see the connection between Faust's present intimacy with Nature and the yearnings of the opening
scene, but only as the resurgence of old frustrations (*3277*).
In his own fashion, too, he is right to think he has cured those
longings (*3269*), though he is quite unaware of the nature of
the medicine. Most importantly, he is right to remind Faust
that the cure for those early speculations, whose natural end
would have been suicide, has been provided by the magical
energies released by the wager (*3270–1*). Faust could have
been protected from the need to make the wager, and could
be protected now from its consequences, only by a capacity
for renunciation which would enable him to withdraw from
Gretchen for ever, and so preserve intact, in this life, the
supreme good that the moment of self-denying love between
these two incompatible beings has revealed. Unprotected by
the ability permanently to renounce, Faust sees the gifts
of love and Nature wither at the touch of the magical,
Mephistophelean, power of negativity which enabled him to
receive those gifts in the first place. For behind both Faust's
love and his life-giving communion with Nature lies, in
Mephistopheles' view, a single force: not the creative
generosity of life but the onward drive of selfish lust.

Mephistopheles has his own notion of what is meant by the
bosom of a friend, or the breasts of Nature (*3336–7*). The
feelings that are concealed beneath the original sensual
imagery with which Faust expressed his yearnings and that
now underlie his pantheistic ecstasies (*3282–91*) are simply the

forces that are driving together Gretchen (*3303–23*) and Faust (*3328–9*) as they have always driven together male and female (*3339*). Any belief that they represent something higher is a self-delusion (*3298*) which merely inhibits the whole-hearted pursuit of pleasure (*3342–4, 3366–73*). But in his encouragements to frank animality and in his seductive picturing of the love-sick Gretchen, Mephistopheles has his own deceitful purpose, revealed not to Faust but to us in an aside (*3325*): the moral corruption of Faust through the self-deception he is pretending to dispel.

Faust's last speech already shows that Mephistopheles has made considerable progress towards his goal. Faust has slid away from the moment when he seemed nearest to denying himself and revoking the wager, and is beginning to lend his own body to Mephistopheles' purposes. He still has sufficient detachment to recognise the difference between his nature and Gretchen's (*3345–55*) and the disaster that must ensue if he yields to his desire. But already he is working himself up to believe the convenient half-truth – that Gretchen is already so distressed by his intrusion on her life that it is too late for renunciation to have any effect, that catastrophe for both of them is inevitable because it has, more or less, happened already (*3356–65*): Gretchen 'had to' be ruined, Hell 'had to' have its victim.

Lines 3374–413 (P150–1, E127–8)

The love between Faust and Gretchen is essentially and exclusively personal. It is love in abstraction from history, society and religion, all of which condition Gretchen, but from all of which Faust has emancipated himself. It expresses itself therefore pre-eminently in monologue, in states of isolation or separation. Dialogue requires, and establishes, a context of shared assumptions, and in *Faust* dialogue between the lovers is usually directed ironically towards showing how inadequate any such social agreement would be to explaining or containing their love. But in monologue, in *Evening*, or in *Forest, Cavern*, for example, or now in *Gretchen's Room*, the

emotion speaks in isolation from any context, even from its
occasion, which may be past or even future, or spatially distant. But the musing self is not alone with its feelings. A tension grows up between the solitary lovers, communing with
each other in absence, in the only medium left to them, a
medium of pure negation, beyond history, society and
religion. And always there is a background, an objective cor-
relative to the feeling – to which, however, it is mysteriously
and symbolically, rather than causally, linked: Gretchen combing her hair; the grandeur of the forest landscape; later we
will have the flowers before the Madonna, the *Dies Irae* at an
unnamed Requiem; and here we have Gretchen at her
spinning-wheel. Its repetitive motion is reflected in the
obsessively recurrent burden of her song, in the unyielding
circle of inescapable desire, now directly voiced, even to the
point of awareness of its affinity with death (*3412–13*). Gretchen's love for Faust is a mystery, its generosity unprompted
by any definable features of its object. The features of her
lover that Gretchen lists are accordingly very generalised
(*3394–401*). None the less they are recognisably the features
that captivate her and arouse our sympathy: nobility of mien,
power of intellect and, above all, of words, and passion (cp.
2680–2, 3187, 3211–12). Gretchen's own sensuality has
awoken. She is no longer the 'good and innocent child' over
whom Mephistopheles claimed to have no power (*3007,
2626*), and his control over events is increasing. The spirit of
negation is familiar in his own way with loneliness and longing, and he now proves to have given in *Forest, Cavern* an
eerie anticipation of Gretchen's dream-like repetitions and
her recourse to song (*3315–23*).

Martha's Garden is probably, in the strict sense of the term,
the most dramatic scene in the entire play, since in it we see
the interaction of two fully developed and mutually independent personalities, and indeed the collision of their worlds.
The incompatibility of Faust and Gretchen, hinted at ever
more explicitly in earlier scenes, is here acted out before our
eyes in the medium of a discussion about religion. The

modern, post-Christian, world represented by Faust and the Christian world represented by Gretchen confront each other directly; it becomes clear that the negativity with which Faust is so inextricably involved precludes any outcome to their relationship other than tragedy.

Lines 3414–25 (P151–2, E128–9)

A new level of intimacy is indicated by Gretchen's use of Faust's Christian name (*3414, 3508*). For the first time we learn that this Faust's name is not the traditional 'Johann' but 'Heinrich'. Goethe may have changed the name because he wished to avoid any easy identification of Faust with himself; or because the name Johann, being widespread among the servant-class, would have comic rather than tragic overtones; or because Heinrich had chivalric and Germanic associations which made it suitable, for example, as a name for figures in ballads. Whatever his reason for changing the name, Goethe needed to place it prominently at some point so as to prepare the way for Gretchen's cry with which the play concludes and which her present use of the name chillingly prefigures. The personal intimacy between the two lovers, established by Gretchen's form of address, contrasts immediately with the historical, social and ideological distance illuminated by her question, 'What about your religion?' (*3415*). Gretchen is as much at home with her social, historical and religious context as Faust is alienated, or emancipated, from his. She recognises instinctively that here lies the obstacle to the closer union between them that they both now desire. Faust is aware of the obstacle too but has, in *Forest, Cavern*, resolved to ignore it. His replies, even to Gretchen's first request, are accordingly cautious, tolerant, sceptical – in short, evasive. But Gretchen is not to be put off.

Lines 3426–31 (P152, E129)

Margarete. [. . .]
                    Glaubst du an Gott?
Faust.
                              Mein Liebchen, wer darf sagen:

Ich glaub' an Gott?
Magst Priester oder Weise fragen,
Und ihre Antwort scheint nur Spott
Über den Frager zu sein.

Margarete.   So glaubst du nicht?
Faust.   Misshör mich nicht, du holdes Angesicht!

(*Margarete.* Do you believe in God? *Faust.* My dear, who has the right to say: I believe in God? Ask priests or wise men, and their answer will only seem a mockery of the questioner. *Margarete.* So you do not believe in Him? *Faust.* Do not misunderstand me, my sweet.)

Gretchen not only arrives at the central question, she formulates it as a dilemma, as two unadorned and incompatible alternatives. If the lovers' relationship is not to founder in such mutual exclusion, Faust must find a way of mediating between the alternatives that is acceptable also to Gretchen. But it must be doubtful whether any compromise will be free of mental reservation on Faust's part. The pose of modesty in the refusal to answer Gretchen positively (as of one who does not 'have the right' to do so) is quickly belied by the truculence that omits the personal pronoun in its demonstrative plain speaking (*3428*). And out of the terms of endearment liberally distributed throughout Faust's speeches in this scene there speaks an embarrassed condescension, affection distanced by an unshaken confidence in social and intellectual superiority. Gretchen, after all, is chided (*3431*) for intellectual unsubtlety. In addition to 'my dear' and 'my sweet' (literally: 'you pretty face', which, it is implied, is all Gretchen is) we have already had 'my child' (*3418*), and shall shortly hear 'dear child' (*3469*), 'dear little doll' (*3476*), 'angel' (*3494*, *3510*) and 'darling' (*3516*). The scene had opened in madrigal verse, to which, after an interlude in *Knittelvers*, always suggestive of rugged unproblematic emotions (*3418–25*), it now returns, but enjambment and caesura in the last lines of Faust's little speech herald the unrhymed free verses that are to come (*3429–30* cp. *3455–6*).

Lines 3432–7 (P152, E129)

Wer darf ihn nennen?
Und wer bekennen:
Ich glaub' ihn.
Wer empfinden,
Und sich unterwinden
Zu sagen: ich glaub' ihn nicht?

(Who has the right to name him? And who to confess: I believe in him. Who to feel and take upon himself to say: I do not believe in him?)

The transition to the new verse-form is at once seamless and exquisitely orderly. The short two-stressed lines are established while the madrigal rhyme-scheme is still running on. The unrhymed lines, of one and three stresses respectively, take up each of Gretchen's alternatives and make of them complementary components of a satisfying rhythmical whole. Both are subordinated syntactically to the opening, emphatically modest, question, 'Who has the right to name him?', which provides the main verb for all that follows. Faust's eloquence has reduced two incompatibles to a unity: he has substituted for Gretchen's questions about the objects of belief a question about the subjective constitution and entitlement of the believer. He will now seek to evoke that unity-in-subjectivity in the passionate free verse we have so far heard only in his declaration of love and his conjuration of the Spirit of Earth. We may therefore be certain that what he says, in its deviousness as in its passion, represents the inmost truth of his nature.

Lines 3438–50 (P152–3, E129)

Der Allumfasser,
Der Allerhalter,
Fasst und erhält er nicht
Dich, mich, sich selbst?
Wölbt sich der Himmel nicht dadroben?
Liegt die Erde nicht hierunten fest?
Und steigen freundlich blickend
Ewige Sterne nicht herauf?

> Schau' ich nicht Aug' in Auge dir,
> Und drängt nicht alles
> Nach Haupt und Herzen dir,
> Und webt in ewigem Geheimnis
> Unsichtbar sichtbar neben dir?

(The all-embracer, the all-sustainer, does he not grasp and sustain you, me, himself? Does not the sky arch over us? Is the earth not firm down here beneath? And do not eternal stars rise up with friendly gaze? Do I not look at you eye to eye and do not all things strain towards your face and heart and live and move in eternal mystery invisibly visible beside you?)

The two-stressed lines are resumed in a sentence whose question-form is at first concealed, as if Faust were now, after disposing of Gretchen's dilemma, embarking on a statement of the true content of his own belief; indeed the hymnic rhythm is reminiscent of the Spirit of Earth's dithyrambic proclamation of its identity (e.g. *506–7*). But that rhythm stumbles slightly (*3440*) and goes over into three- and four-stressed lines as if Faust cannot contain what he has to say within so restricted a metre, just as he cannot maintain the form of simple statement. The question-structure of his opening lines is taken up once more and, once established, varied and extended with almost musical virtuosity: first single parallel verses (*3442–3*), then an extension to two lines, introduced by *und* (*3444–5*), then a repetition of this single-plus-double pattern (*3446–8*), extended by a further two-line unit (*3449–50*) as the questions gather momentum. The significance of this gravitation away from statement into question is betrayed when the rhythm stumbles as the sentence structure changes and Faust lists the objects of the sustaining divine embrace (*3440–1*): in first and most emphatic position comes not God, nor even Faust, but Gretchen, *dich* What is foremost in his mind emerges first, and with it his reason for adopting a sentence-form, not of statement, but of urgent personal appeal. These are not formulations of theological belief but attempts at persuasion – and not just theological persuasion either. The firm and ordered structure to earth and heaven, the frame of rest for the motion of stars, might seem to recall Faust's vision of the macrocosm, but already the words *dadroben* and *hierunten* ('up above', 'here below') contain a suggestion of the personal viewpoint of Gretchen that is being made the centre of the universe, a suggestion which becomes explicit in the mention of the stars' benevolent involvement. Their friendly gaze provides the transition to Faust's own gaze, directed like every word he utters only at that single central point, and interpreted by him as continuous and harmonious with the fundamental order and energy of the world. When, in a line which bears great emphasis through its return to the original two-stressed pattern, Faust is seeking a word for this orientation of all things on Gretchen, he chooses the word *drängt* ('strains'), used in the previous scene by Gretchen herself in an unashamedly sexual sense (*3406*). This 'credo' of Faust's, his rejection of a simply objective theology for a vision of a world-order at once objective and totally personalised, equally material and spiritual, 'invisibly visible', is an immensely sophisticated exercise in the art of seduction.

It is of course not only that. Faust is not, like the hero of the young Goethe's farce *Satyros*, a lecher who ensnares his victims in a web of melodious metaphysical words. It is by reference to religion that Faust has defined his modernity, and so his incompatibility with Gretchen, and the theology he puts forward is not arbitrary – it is itself historically specific. In 1781 G. C. Tobler, a visitor to the Weimar court, wrote a brief essay summarising the pantheistic Nature-worship he found prevailing there:

Nature! We are surrounded by her, engulfed in her . . . each of her works has a being of its own, each manifestation is a unique conception, and yet they all make one . . . Every moment she begins an unending race and every moment she is at the goal . . . She has neither speech nor language: but she creates hearts and voices, and in them she feels and speaks. Love is her crown . . .

Except for one point, the theological content of this essay does not differ from that of Faust's speech: surrounding and engulfing Nature, the all-embracer, whose motions are eternal and yet identical with the longings and actions of the unique finite beings of which the world is composed; the love between creatures as the self-expression of the central energy in the universe. There is of course every difference between Tobler's unstructured sequence of flat antitheses and cryptic banalities, which T. S. Eliot found 'as dismal as a rural sermon', and Goethe's incomparably greater rhetorical resourcefulness: the varying lengths, types and rhythms of his sentences, his concentration on simple but forceful verbs, his avoidance of dead or half-dead metaphor and instead his use in an unexpected context of adverbs familiar in themselves ('friendly', 'invisibly'), his sparing decoration of an unpretentious vocabulary with an occasional, possibly neologistic, compound (e.g. 'der Allumfasser'), which in German is likely to be both more lucid and more natural than its English equivalent − a style in fact which combines the unpredictable inventiveness and chaste vigour of Dante with the endlessly subtle sensuous associativeness of Shakespeare.

But the principal difference between the utterances of the poet and the would-be philosopher lies somewhere else: in the dramatic medium into which the (possibly rather commonplace) ideas of the time have been inserted. In *Faust* the ideas are shown to us in use, active in human lives, active as Goethe must have felt them to be, at least to some extent, in his own time and place: they are the ideas supremely characteristic of Faust himself, as the play's opening scene has shown, and to hold such ideas, we now see, *is* to want to seduce Gretchen. The ideas occasion and illuminate a conflict of personalities and loyalties, but Faust is also using them, as he expresses them, in an attempt to resolve, or at any rate conceal, the conflict. His sensual motive for this, long implicit in his rhetoric, declares itself at last in action: he is now doing what he has long been saying (cp. *456, 1750, 3221, 3288*). We have seen a similar interplay of philosophy and psychology in the monologues that led up to the suicide attempt and the wager, or in Faust's last speech of self-justification in *Forest, Cavern*. (See T. S. Eliot's account of Shakespeare's similar procedure in 'Shakespeare and the Stoicism of Seneca', *Selected Essays* (London, 1951), pp. 126–40.) *Faust* is not just a philosophical poem, a work in which the expression of philosophy is subordinate to poetic ends, but a dramatic poem, a work in which a principal poetic effect is dramatic collision – and irony.

Lines 3451–8 (P153, E129)

Erfüll davon dein Herz, so gross es ist,
Und wenn du ganz in dem Gefühle selig bist,
Nenn es dann, wie du willst,
Nenn's Glück! Herz! Liebe! Gott!
Ich habe keinen Namen
Dafür! Gefühl ist alles:
Name ist Schall und Rauch
Umnebelnd Himmelsglut.

(Fill your heart with this, great as it is, and when you are completely blissful in that feeling, then call it what you will, call it happiness, heart, love, God! I have no name for it. Feeling is everything – names are sound and smoke, clouding heaven's fire.)

The change from questions to imperatives marks the climax in Faust's ever-more-manifest concentration of his thoughts on Gretchen. The brief recurrence of rhyme in a nearly regular iambic pentameter couplet not only identifies the weightiest utterance in the whole speech, as far as Faust is concerned, but reminds us of the opening madrigal verses and so of the questions from which Faust began. This then is his answer: not a statement, but an appeal to Gretchen to make her own the exclusively subjectivist state of mind in which he started his odyssey and in which the only God acknowledged was the God who dwelt in his breast. The original suggestion that he should give a name to this state is an anticlimax tersely dismissed in an unrhymed line of prosaic monosyllables (*3453*), and in the list of possible names now reeled off with apparent indifference there is one notable omission which constitutes the single discrepancy between Faust's theology and Tobler's. Faust says nothing of Nature: his sojourn in the forest cavern is now far behind him. Nature is a thing, not a feeling; to mention Nature at all would be a concession to objectivity; and by putting God in the same series as happiness, the heart and love, Faust wishes to imply that Gretchen's God is a feeling too. Into the very expression of his frustrated indifference, however, Faust inserts the point of the whole tirade: among the possible synonyms for the supreme sustaining reality is 'love'. The object of his own yearning and the God who for Gretchen is the highest value can both perhaps bear the same name.

There is here the ironic comedy of the Don Juan, or the Tartuffe, who denies an interest in words at the moment when he has deliberately let fall the most important word of all. There is also the more complex irony that the entire speech has sought to express poetically an assault on the foundation of poetry, on the importance of words. The search is paradoxically successful: the sound and smoke of Faust's outburst against names culminates in the naming of the unforgettable image of the sun obscured, the only metaphor in the speech. By its very vividness that metaphor obscures from our view the devious rhetoric that has preceded. Psychologically speaking, it is associated with the mood of smouldering resentment in which Faust wishes Gretchen to think he is left after the violence words have done to his feelings. These words against words also proclaim their historical location: their vocabulary belongs as clearly to the movement of Sentimentalism as their elliptical syntax belongs to Storm and Stress. And history provides another irony for which Goethe is not directly responsible but which goes to the heart of the contradiction in Faust's nature: 'feeling is all' are words which in German culture have subsequently become an intellectual's cliché.

Lines 3459–61 (P153, E130)

Margarete.   Das ist alles recht schön und gut;
Ungefähr sagt das der Pfarrer auch,
Nur mit ein bisschen andern Worten.

(*Margarete.* That is all quite all right; the priest more or less says that too, only the words are a bit different.)

This is the point of collision, a moment of Shakespearean

complexity. Suddenly another voice cuts across Faust's bewit-
chingly involuted monologue and, for all his ambition to be
all-embracing, he becomes but a part of a larger world. The
last two lines of his irregular unrhymed monologue are taken
up into the rhyme-scheme of Gretchen's madrigal verse. The
recondite and literary sentences in which Faust has affirmed
his closeness to wordless reality are put in their place by the
simple colloquialisms of that 'ordinary language' whose
perfectly precise vagueness is the despair of philosophers. Not
that Gretchen is naive. She understands that Faust's religious
assertion contains a declaration of love, but concludes after
a little pondering − hence the initial vagueness − that it can
be identified with what her own religion tells her of the relation between divine and human love. There is of course a hint
of comedy in the assimilation of Faust's position to that of
the greedy cleric who 'digested' Faust's first gift of jewels,
but the implied discrepancy is not necessarily only comic.
Gretchen is right: Faust's assertion that God is unnameable,
omnipresent, and identical with Love, has a theological tradition behind it at least as old as Christianity itself. But we
know, as Gretchen does not know, at any rate consciously,
that Faust's reasons for making these assertions are not those
of the authorities, both religious and social, which Gretchen
acknowledges. We have been aware, at least since Faust
translated St John, that any coincidence between Faust's
religious terminology and that of tradition exists only during
his good pleasure and by his authority. Again, there is a
superficial comedy in the suggestion that Faust's passionate
rhetoric is only 'slightly' different from the language of a
Sunday sermon. But beneath that comedy lies a bewildering
and potentially tragic irony. Gretchen says that the difference
between Faust and the Church is 'only' a difference of words.
In that, it seems, she comes to an agreement with Faust, a
compromise between the terms of the dilemma she first posed.
Faust, after all, has also just asserted, however paradoxically,
that words do not matter. But while for Faust *all* words are
sound and smoke, stifling the fire in his breast, for Gretchen
the words of the priest, like any ordinary words, have some

have some flexibility because they 'do not matter' as much as the things which they signify — in this case, the divine truths to which they approximate. The illusion of an agreement is possible because for Faust words are trivial, while for Gretchen they are elastic. But we, the audience, see through that illusion and for us the words of this dramatic exchange are crystal clear and hard: the illusory compromise which will enable Faust and Gretchen to come together reveals to us that their worlds are irreconcilable.

Lines 3462–5 (P153, E130)

Faust.   Es sagen's allerorten
Alle Herzen unter dem himmlischen Tage,
Jedes in seiner Sprache;
Warum nicht ich in der meinen?

(*Faust.* It is said everywhere by all hearts under the light of heaven, each in its own language; why not I in mine?)

Faust re-enters fully into the flow of dialogue, two of his madrigal lines rhyming outside the confines of his speech, and he maintains a conciliatory tone. He echoes in fact the universal sympathies of the young Herder, for whom the endless variety of human culture and language was a polyphonous chorus of praise to God. Faust's plea to be regarded as but one voice in that chorus gains an agreeable immediacy from his use of the Frankfurt dialect, Goethe's own, in rhyming 'Tage' and 'Sprache'. But the plea is specious, for Faust's claim, in his ecstatic 'credo', as throughout the play, has not been that he is one voice among many in the wealth of human cultural history, one particular dialect of the human language, but that he is above and beyond historical, cultural and linguistic restriction altogether. His final question is rhetorical and does not really expect an answer.

Gretchen, however, is not finally won over — not here or later — by a tempting compromise that she herself has helped to formulate. She recognises that Faust's apparently conciliatory pluralism conceals a claim not to be bound by the specific religious and historical terms in which God has revealed Himself to her and her milieu: 'you're still not a proper Christian'. The loose colloquialism of her couplet (*3466–8*) concludes with quiet emphasis an argument which, in abstract terms, can be taken no further.

Lines 3469–543 (P153–6, E130–3)

More than any other scene in the play, *Martha's Garden* demonstrates the unity of Goethe's original conception, the inseparability of the story of Faust the magician and the story of Faust the lover. In his 'credo' we see the language of the magus, of the man who flung open Nostradamus' secret book, being bent to the purposes of love – purposes perhaps natural to it anyway. In the remainder of the scene the conflict between the worlds of Faust and Gretchen, which the 'credo' revealed, is elaborated dramatically in the form of the tension between Gretchen and Mephistopheles, the magician's traditional companion. Gretchen's instinct carries her on, with unerring logic, to the source of all that is un-Christian in the man she loves. In Mephistopheles she recognises the enemy of her religion (*3498*), of her morality (*3481*) and above all of love, even of her love for Faust (*3497*), of which she gives a particularly tender evocation (*3491–2*):

> Es steht ihm an der Stirn geschrieben,
> Dass er nicht mag eine Seele lieben.   (*3489–90*)

(It is written all over his face that he could not love a soul.)

The conflict between Faust and Gretchen now appears as a conflict in their interpretation of Mephistopheles' character, and if in the first part of the scene Faust seemed to have the broader intellectual scope, he now seems guilty of a deliberate self-deception, closing himself to Gretchen's deeper insight into the true nature and intentions of his partner, and consoling her with soothing and condescending platitudes (*3483*, *3501*). His elaborately periphrastic proposal that they should spend the night together contrasts unfavourably with Gretchen's immediate and practical understanding of the matter (*3502–9*).

Before our eyes Mephistopheles' influence now extends further, reaching out into Gretchen's family as Faust gives her the sleeping-draught that will quieten her watchful mother and make their assignation possible. The draught clearly comes from the Spirit of Lies, as certainly does Faust's appeal to Gretchen to trust him to do nothing dangerous (*3516*). So when Mephistopheles himself appears, both his devilish nature and his power are frighteningly enhanced. He has overheard all the preceding conversation: Gretchen's concern to draw Faust into the social order he interprets as the self-interest of a Mistress Martha (*3525–7*). His hostility towards Gretchen increases, he speaks as slightingly as he can of her intuitive understanding of him, and when he tells Faust that he will take his own kind of pleasure in the doings of the coming night his cruelty and perversity are manifest. Faust however seems impervious to the horrible thought that Gretchen is about to be delivered into the power of one whom she fears, and who will encompass and relish the destruction of all she loves.

Lines 3544–86 (P156–8, E133–5)

The social order, then, is not simply a refuge which Gretchen can offer a storm-tossed Faust. It too is partially allied with Mephistopheles. In *At the Well* Gretchen begins to confront the social powers which forbid her love for Faust. Even so the scene is close to monologue, to which it reverts, for Lieschen and her friends play no further part in the plot. They and their cruel gossip, to which Mistress Martha has already referred (*3197–201*), simply represent the social world symbolised in the background image of the well, the place of public meeting. That world will be as merciless as Mephistopheles towards its victim. Gretchen, however makes no attempt to exculpate herself: she accepts that the same judgement that applies to the used and abandoned Barbara applies also to her, and it does not cross her mind to dispute the rightfulness of the social and religious tribunal before which she will stand accused (cp. *2949*). She has no changed since she showed that it was as natural to her to want the jewels Faust left her as to accept with sadness that they belonged to someone else. So now, despite the anguish it causes her, she will neither reject the moral convention that condemns her nor brand her love as wrong.

Lines 3587–619 (P158–9, E135–6)

The religious determinants of Gretchen's identity are specifically Catholic: frequent confession, prayers for the dead, deference to the priesthood, and devotion to the Virgin. (However Protestant the play as a whole may be, there is in *Faust* no place for, or interest in, Protestantism as such: its religious poles are Catholicism and pagan secularism; there is no middle path.) Gretchen's acceptance of social and moral determinacy culminates in her submission to the religion of the Cross, which in the Mater Dolorosa, Our Lady of Sorrows, provides a transfigured image of her suffering. The symbolic background to a monologue enters here into a direct relation with the speaker. But Gretchen's prayer before the Madonna's shrine, in an unfrequented alley between the houses and the town wall, is not just an image. It is a turning-point in her life. It is immaterial which of her own Calvaries – her discovery of her pregnancy, the death of her mother, her fear of abandonment by Faust – provides the occasion for this prayer, and Goethe does not tell us. What matters is that she accepts in torment the agonies of the 'constricted' life – sin, guilt, shame, punishment and, even worse, the fear of all these – as earlier she gratefully accepted its simple rewards. She does not do as Faust did and curse the circumstances of her life, but pours her suffering into the forms of worship and anguished supplication that her life has always held ready for her. Despite the expressively irregular metre of her lines their rhyme-scheme is strict and strongly reminiscent both of the medieval sequence, the *Stabat mater*, to which explicit allusion is made, and of the forms and language of seventeenth-century German hymnody. And because Gretchen in her own moment of sadness unto death

does not relinquish or despair of the very world that is cruci-
fying her, the way will also be open for her to receive redemption through the forms and channels which the constricted life
has always held ready too.

Lines 3620–775 (P159–64, E136–42)

The remorseless approach of public shame is the theme with
which the night scene in front of Gretchen's door begins and
ends. Gretchen's soldier brother Valentin, a boastful fellow
whose emotions are as coarse as the *Knittelvers* he speaks, is
something of a male equivalent to Lieschen and regards his
sister as a piece of valuable property. Rumours of the love
affair injure his own standing, and he resolves on
characteristically violent revenge, if not at Faust's expense,
then at Gretchen's. Both from Valentin's remarks and from
what Faust himself says (*3674–5*), it is clear that Faust is now
a frequent nocturnal visitor to Gretchen. Faust's mood of
uneasy despondency (*3650–4*) may have several roots: the
despair into which we have more than once seen him sink
after a moment of ecstasy; the awareness that retribution is
closing in on Gretchen; most profoundly perhaps the recognition of his now nearly total dependence on Mephistopheles,
to which the central episode in the scene is devoted.

For Mephistopheles, by contrast with Faust, is throughout
sprightly and in command, looking forward to the coming
Walpurgis Night, the celebration of the evil that now
permeates the play (*3661* cp. *2590* – the present scene takes
place on the night of 28 April). The gradual process by which
he has usurped Faust's identity and extended his influence
into every part of his life reaches a horrible culmination as he
takes over even Faust's role as lover and serenades Gretchen
with a cruel and scornful song. The song is adapted from one
of Ophelia's and perhaps suggests that Gretchen will receive
from Faust little better treatment than Ophelia did from
Hamlet. In the duel with Valentin, Mephistopheles' moral
domination of Faust is at its height: Mephistopheles arranges
that, while it is he who makes Faust's victory easy, it is Faust

who has the responsibility for the lethal blow, and, instead of defending himself in equal combat, Faust appears as the craven murderer of a paralysed man. Faust's cowardliness is underlined by the disappearance of the partners in crime, who are now outlawed from human society and leave Gretchen to face public recrimination alone. Gretchen has to watch her brother die, killed by the man she loves, and has to endure his brutal denunciation of her, knowing it to be well founded. When she cries out 'what pains of Hell!' (*3770*) she is uttering the literal truth: she has begun to feel the pains which the spirit of Hell rejoices to inflict on his victims.

Lines 3776–834 (P165–6, E142–4)

For Gretchen, the ultimate pain would be to know herself rejected by the divine power for which she has lived and in which she has taken refuge. The insidious temptation to that final despair is whispered in her ear by an evil spirit in the scene *Cathedral*, while the choir, representing the full weight of religious and social condemnation, sing, in the *Dies Irae*, of the Last Day, of the revelation of hidden crimes, and of the severity of divine judgement. The verses sung − or rather heard, for we are in Gretchen's mind − are selected for their appropriateness to her condition. Responsible now, directly or indirectly, for the deaths of her brother and her mother (the victim of the doubtless Mephistophelean sleeping-draught), she knows that, invisible as yet to the world, a child is growing within her. The pain of remorse and of the memory of lost innocence is, like all pain, of diabolical origin, and as it grips her Gretchen must fear she is falling into the hands of her enemy. Yet the fear and the pain are inseparable from the religion which she will not abandon: the constricted life has become spiritually and physically crushing, asphyxiating (*3810*, *3816–20*). Only in one line, the last, are we released from the torture-chamber of Gretchen's consciousness into the prosaic reality − in this trans-historical drama, be it noted, an eighteenth-century reality − of the bottle of smelling-salts. In order perhaps to intensify the privacy of

Gretchen's suffering Goethe decided not to retain his original specification that the Requiem concerned was that of Gretchen's mother. That would have forced on Gretchen the public role of principal mourner and have confused the poetic effect of our concentration on her solitary agony. The real public world glimpsed briefly in that last line will soon enough be a place of torment for Gretchen: the smelling-bottle is like the first touch of a waking reality in which the terrors of the night are not dispersed. But with this scene the depiction of Gretchen's private martyrdom is complete — the mechanics of the public process could not add to it. After her final swoon, we, the readers, shall not see Gretchen again, except as the condemned prisoner on the eve of execution.

Chapter 6

Tragedy

(*Walpurgis Night – Walpurgis Night's Dream – Dark Day, Countryside – Night, Open Country – Prison*)

Faust and Mephistopheles climb the Brocken to take part in the Witches' Sabbath on Walpurgis Night. In the midst of degradation Faust is distracted by a vision of Gretchen, which Mephistopheles attempts to efface from his mind by entertaining him with the political and intellectual obsessions of Goethe's own time. Faust awakens to the knowledge that in his absence Gretchen has killed her child, for fear of scandal, and has been imprisoned and condemned to death. He insists on making a rescue attempt but finds Gretchen partly deranged, and with thoughts only for her crimes. Mephistopheles appears, warning that dawn is approaching, and demanding that they leave immediately: Gretchen recoils in horror from her old enemy and refuses to come with Faust, for that would put her too in the Devil's hands. She entrusts herself instead to the judgement of Heaven, which pronounces her redeemed. Mephistopheles disappears, taking Faust with him.

The shock of the transition from Gretchen's agony in the cathedral to Mephistopheles' crassly frivolous enquiry whether Faust would not prefer to ride up the mountains on a broomstick is a *coup de théâtre* equalled only by the transition out of the *Walpurgis Night's Dream* into *Dark Day, Countryside*. Two explanations of this astonishing discord are possible, though they might at first seem contradictory. First, in entering into his bond with Mephistopheles, Faust, to whom the life beyond good and evil lived by the Spirit of Earth proved inaccessible, has chosen negativity in a human form and on a human scale: he has chosen evil. The nature of that choice is now made apparent in a scene which, like *Forest, Cavern*, is not so much a dramatic as a poetic and meditative development of the implications of what has immediately preceded. In abandoning or forgetting Gretchen in her moment of greatest need, Faust has reached the lowest point in his moral career, a point marked by the shock of transition with which the scene begins. As he climbs the mountains, Faust does not penetrate further into depravity. It is simply made more manifest to us that *this* is his choice, *this* is the alternative to Gretchen: near-enslavement to Mephistopheles and nearly complete self-deception. Structurally speaking, as the story of Faust and Gretchen nears its denouement, *Walpurgis Night* reflects the world of ideas and emotions in which Faust made the wager that is now tearing the lovers apart, a world which we last saw in its true colours in *Witch's Kitchen*. Second, however, it is in keeping with the Shakespearean manner of the play to interrupt the emotionally most taxing scenes with an interlude of comic relief, rather as the scenes with the grave-diggers and Osric preface the tragic conclusion of *Hamlet*.

The paradox that Faust's nearest approach to pure evil is treated in a predominantly comic and satirical tone can, however, be resolved. The Walpurgis Night is the world of deceit and illusion: the sensuality, and the intellectual distractions, with which Mephistopheles endeavours to swamp Faust, are as remote from reality as the wager by which Faust bound himself to the spirit of lies in the first place. Like all magic, they are, however damaging their effects, ultimately unserious. The true substance of life was briefly revealed to Faust when he and Gretchen exchanged kisses. There is no substance, no reality, to be found on the Brocken, nor anywhere else in the life Faust leads by virtue of the wager and in separation from Gretchen. But even now that separation is not complete. When Faust is in the depths of stupefaction Gretchen's memory comes to awaken him, and gradually, and with various setbacks, the truth of his condition dawns upon him. Mephistopheles of course seeks to lull Faust's conscience, but in *Dark Day, Countryside* his machinations are revealed, and Faust begins a desperate attempt to undo the consequences of his own actions. From this moment of truth onwards the play accelerates, at the height of emotional tension, into a heartrending recapitulation in *Prison* and a recognition of goodness lost beyond recall. In its mingling of realism and poetry, of despair and hope beyond despair, the last scene is truly and profoundly tragic.

Lines 3835–911 (P167–9, E144–7)

From the mind of Gretchen our attention moves to the mind of Faust, it too holding intercourse with demons, for both lovers are now in the realm of darkness. Goethe is the first writer to link the Faust legend with the old tradition that on the eve of the feast of St Walpurga (1 May) witches foregather on the Brocken, the highest peak of the Harz mountains, to worship Satan in a Black Mass. Less originally, Goethe's treatment of this theme also includes, as did *Study I*, the dramatisation of a German proverbial expression, for wishing something 'to the Brocken' is the equivalent in German of wishing something 'to the Devil' in English. In 1798 the satirist G. C. Lichtenberg had published a humorous essay, *To the Devil with You (Dass du auf dem Blocksberge wärst!)*, in which he visits the Brocken and meets whoever and whatever has recently been wished there. There is therefore a basis in tradition for the elements of contemporary satire which make Goethe's scene puzzling and opaque for the modern reader but which fulfil one of the main purposes of the poem: Goethe's reckoning up with the intellectual world of his own time (see Chapter 1, section III), with what, in a preparatory note for *Walpurgis Night*, he called 'current German mischief' ('jetzigen Unfug in Deutschland'). Although most of the scene was written around 1800, and this is the period which the satirical allusions reflect, Goethe's plans for a *Walpurgis Night* go back at least to 1775, when his friend J. M. R. Lenz wrote a somewhat similar literary satire, *Pandämonium Germanikum*, situated on a German Parnassus (cp. *4317*) rather than the Brocken. This is likely to have been as significant a model as Lichtenberg's essay.

That Faust is still not totally 'endevilled' (*3371*) is shown by his appreciating a walk by natural means through the spring night, a remote echo of *Forest, Cavern* (*3838–47*), but when Mephistopheles summons a will-o'-the-wisp to speed their progress they enter 'the sphere of dreams and magic' (*3871*) and hallucination begins (*3906–11*). Faint recollections of past love and happiness remain (*3884–8*).

Lines 3912–4015 (P169–73, E147–50)

Reaching an intermediate peak (*3913*) the wanderers experience two great manifestations of worldly evil: money and sex both of which have played their part in betraying Gretchen into the hands of the Devil. On this night all the mineral gold, in which the Harz is rich, glows through the ground as if the palace of Mammon were being illuminated (*3932–3*), a Miltonic reminiscence. Then a gale, the mythical 'bride of the winds' (*3936*), sweeps in a swarm of witches and wizards, singing in raucous antiphony of bestial sexuality, including, hideously, infanticide and abortion (*3976–7*), and settling like locusts on the moors. An important chronological allusion tells us that the scene is situated at the time of the French Revolution, which Goethe regarded as the fulfilment of the anti-humanist barbarism initiated by the Protestant Reformation (*3996–9*).

Lines 4016–95 (P173–6, E150–3)

The setting of the Walpurgis Night resembles an enormous fairground. Acting, as it seems to Faust, out of a spirit of pure contradiction (*4030*), Mephistopheles frustrates Faust's curiosity by plucking him out of the main throng streaming up to Satan's throne and entertaining him instead with a series of sideshows. Faust, now at his nadir, his striving swamped at last (*4037*), professes himself obedient to Mephistopheles' instructions (*4030*). His will is powerless: from this 'endevilment' only an external agency can rescue him. Purporting to explain his contrariness, Mephistopheles refers to the 'course' he intended Faust to follow after the wager: first the little world, and only then the great (*4036*, *4042–5* cp. *2052*). By insinuating that the evil to which Faust has hitherto been a party is a 'little', personal matter, and that there is some grander evil, for which he is supposedly not yet ripe, Mephistopheles is concealing that he himself, and not some spectre higher up the Brocken, is already Satan in Faust's life, in so far as Faust is capable of perceiving, of 'grasping', him (*3866*, *4062–9*). Aesthetically, indeed, *Part One* (strictly understood) can no more appropriately contain a representation of metaphysically absolute Evil than of metaphysically absolute Good – neither is an element in Faust's religious consciousness and both could be directly manifested in his story only as allegories unrelated to his doings. The greatest, most nearly direct, manifestation of evil in his age, Goethe believed, was the French Revolution, and though in many works he represented the indirect consequences of that upheaval he always shied away from a representation of the eruption itself. So here Faust, like many of Goethe's German contemporaries, becomes embroiled in a series of small-scale erotic, intellectual or even political encounters, which all are only marginal sideshows to the full-scale Witches' Sabbath going on elsewhere, in Paris or on the Brocken, but which all are highly effective distractions from the true substance of serious living. Each of these distractions, in this scene and the next, is a representative of the spiritual milieu in which Faust's despair, his curse, and his wager were born – the revolutionary and Romantic world of post-Christian intellectuals, particularly German, and particularly Idealist. This is the solid link which binds these phantoms to the story of Faust's crime against Gretchen. The first such 'club' (*4035*) – a vogue term of the Revolution – is a group of representatives of the *ancien régime*, disgruntled at their displacement by the changing times (*4072–95*).

Lines 4096–222 (P176–80, E153–8)

A great turn in the action now begins: into Faust's Walpurgis Night, his stupefaction by the evil of the little world, a great power for good begins to intervene. Gradually the recollection of Faust's real crimes begins to piece itself together out of the delusions. First, a witch offers for sale wares which all are veiled reminders of what Faust has done: jewellery, such as seduced Gretchen, poison, such as killed her mother, weapons, such as treacherously killed Valentin (*4100–9*). No wonder Mephistopheles hurries Faust away, assuring the witch that Faust is not interested in the past, only in novelties (*4110–13*). Faust himself faintly registers the danger of losing his identity completely in the throng pushing on from stall to stall (*4114–15*). There follow three encounters with erotically charged female images, of increasingly sharp definition: first Lilith, a generalised figure of female sexuality (*4118–23*), then a young witch, with whom Faust engages in an orgiastic dance whose nature is fully revealed by its parody in a dance between Mephistopheles and an older witch (*4124–43*). A distorted form of reason, a caricature of the Berlin popular philosopher Friedrich Nicolai, endeavours to intervene but is as ludicrously out of place in this debauch as was Nicolai's rationalist Enlightenment (*4159*) in the age of Idealism (*4166*) and the Revolution. Faust breaks off his dance before it becomes the symbolic consummation of his betrayal of Gretchen, because his partner is revealed as a phantasm, even a corpse (*4178–9*), and because a third image has finally brought Gretchen and his past clearly before his eyes. Recollections of real love of a living body penetrate the haze of deceit and perversion (*4197–8*), but chains round the vision's feet and a thin red line round her neck foreshadow her fate. This is the moment when Faust's conscience awakens, identical with the moment of his greatest intimacy with evil, for it is the one occasion in the play when Faust calls Mephistopheles by his name, and in an abbreviated, familiar form at that (*4183*). Even though Faust's mind is now open only to images of naked, dead and disfigured flesh, in which therefore the good and holy must clothe itself, if it is to reach him, the memory of Gretchen's love has come to fetch him back from the very forecourts of Hell. Mephistopheles once more dismisses these stirrings of conscience, variously reinterpreting the vision as a Medusa (*4194, 4208*) and an all-purpose succubus (*4200*), and blusteringly seeks to divert Faust with the ultimate unreality, a dream within a dream (*4209–22*).

Lines 4223–398 (P181–6, E158–63)

The 'Intermezzo', as Goethe calls it, of the *Walpurgis Night's Dream* struck nineteenth-century critics as an alien intrusion in Faust's drama, but a modern sensibility, used to the tonal contrasts and collage techniques of Eliot and Pound, will not find it strange. As its title and sub-title imply, it dilutes the devilry of the Walpurgis Night into the comic and fairy world of *A Midsummer Night's Dream*, and so it simultaneously marks Faust's furthest distance from the reality of his and Gretchen's condition and signals that night is far advanced (*4215*) and dawn is approaching. It is, as Mephistopheles indicates (*4221–2*), a satirical review of everything in contemporary Germany that Goethe could wish to the Devil (and Goethe himself makes a brief and sardonic appearance, as the 'Worldling', saying much the same, *4327–30*). The late-eighteenth-century intellectual world, which once seemed so weighty and imposing when it engendered Faust's great wager, is here reduced to inanity. Feuds and coteries of artists and litterateurs (*4259–330*), Idealist philosophers and their enemies (*4331–62*), political time-servers and casualties (*4367–87*), are all dispatched in tripping, witty, quatrains whose purpose in the structure of the play is precisely to appear, with their subject-matter, as an utterly frivolous distraction from real life. We are to forget Gretchen, as Mephistopheles wishes Faust to do. The scene is given a rondo form by the repeated interventions of the bandmaster and his orchestra and by the continual references to grasses, insects and stars which keep before us the picture of a masque or entertainment out of doors on a spring night. Eventually a reference to worn-out dancing-shoes tells us the night is nearly over (4373–4), and the fairy figures who opened the entertainment, Puck and Ariel, return to lead the participants away. A final quatrain, *pianissimo*, from the orchestra varies the landscape imagery into a clear evocation of a time of day – the first breath of morning after the ball. And with that breath all illusions evaporate into the nothingness from which they came; a crowded, noisy dream gives way to the silence of a solitary dawn:

> Wolkenzug und Nebelflor
> Erhellen sich von oben.
> Luft im Laub und Wind im Rohr,
> Und alles ist zerstoben. (4395–8)

(Trains of cloud and veils of mist grow light from above. Breath in the leaves and wind in the reeds and everything is scattered.)

Dark Day, Countryside (P187–9, E164–5)

Into this almost shamefaced silence of wind and rattling reeds bursts the cry with which Faust opens the only scene in *Part One* left in prose. It is the cry of a man awakening to the awareness of having committed some dreadful crime while the victim of an evil intoxication. Gretchen's situation, a prosaic reality as inescapable as the stale and overcast morning, is known to him at last. The Walpurgis Night may have seemed to last but a night, but while he has been rapt in the magic world of illusion many months have passed, perhaps a whole year, and Gretchen has become a criminal, fled, been captured, imprisoned and condemned. (The footnote in the Penguin edition (P167) rests on a misunderstanding of this point in the chronology. All the events of the play from its opening to *Walpurgis Night* can be fitted – just – into the period from Easter to Mayday in a single year. It is in *Walpurgis Night* that the months of Gretchen's pregnancy are to be placed.) Faust's negligent abandonment of Gretchen, like Mephistopheles' comment 'She is not the first', or his earlier remark 'I'll have my own pleasure from it' (3543), is in retrospect far more unmistakably devilish than any of the phantoms on the Brocken. It has of course been

Mephistopheles' intention to 'lull' Faust with 'distractions' and postpone as long as possible this moment of truth, which still comes too early for him. Mephistopheles would rather Faust were still blinding himself to Gretchen's sufferings and his part in bringing them about, and were still dancing with witches, while she is executed. Such a Faust would be much more certainly 'endevilled' than this remorseful, if not actually repentant, sinner who, however late in the day, is now intent on rushing to her aid.

Mephistopheles therefore does all he can to hold Faust back from his intention. He denies that it is within his power to help, and seeks to reduce Faust to inactive despair and acknowledgement of final defeat, by taunting him with his own guilt and by scorning him savagely as a windbag who cannot live up to his own ambitions when they are realised. So much, he says, for the man who wanted to measure himself with the Spirit of Earth in his capacity for creative and destructive experience. And indeed this scene is the final reckoning with Faust, the man of so many self-deceptive words, who has of words such a low opinion. His first speeches reach an extreme of hyperbole as he strains in vain to transfer his guilt to Mephistopheles, under the pretence of expressing his revulsion from what has happened. Then, when Mephistopheles is most literally Satan, the Accuser, and asks 'Who was it that plunged her into ruin? I or you?', Faust for the first time has no answer. He 'looks about him wildly'. Words really do fail him at the very moment when his hubris, of which his hostility to words was an integral part, finally collapses. His remaining speeches are brief and concentrate on the business of the rescue.

Grace came into Faust's life with the enlightenment of his conscience, even in the depths of the Walpurgis Night. In his determination to attempt a rescue he responds to that grace and shows that he is not yet wholly lost. That he is not saved, either, is apparent from his willingness to continue using magical means to effect his purpose. But that Mephistopheles has not yet ultimately got his way we know when he makes his last and feeblest attempt to dissuade Faust from action, on the grounds that such an operation is now too dangerous. Faust in contemptuous fury does not dignify the argument with a reply. Once, in the encounter with Valentin, he may have seemed a coward, and putty in Mephistopheles' hands. Now his courage, almost lost from view since his opening monologue, has returned, Mephistopheles has to capitulate and resume his role as Faust's servant, and the play runs headlong into its final climax.

Lines 4399–404 (P189, E166)

Even as a servant, however, Mephistopheles remains dangerous. The very words in which he agreed to take part in the rescue attempt – 'I shall carry you off' (*ich entführe euch*) – contained a reminder that he who accepts the Devil's assistance puts himself in the Devil's power. The distorting effect of reliance on Mephistopheles' powers is apparent in the mysteriously suggestive vignette of Faust's breakneck ride with him across Germany, *Night, Open Country*. Even though the gibbet which they pass is not identical with the place of execution Gretchen will shortly envisage for herself (*4588–9*), it is clearly poetically essential for it to stand in the closest symbolic relationship to her impending death. Around it Faust sees the movements of spiritual beings. The words he uses to describe them are consistently noble, suggesting beneficence, even homage (they 'strow and bless' and 'bow'), as if he supposed he is seeing angels consecrating a holy spot. Mephistopheles by contrast uses coarse and banal terms, dismissing the apparition as a coven of witches: 'no idea what they're brewing up'. The conflict of interpretations which has been so regular a feature of the converse between Faust and Mephistopheles, most recently in their different responses to the phantom of Gretchen in *Walpurgis Night*, now takes on an ominous, apocalyptic quality. Into the drama which is fast approaching a sombre crisis the spirit world is also being drawn, it cannot yet be said whether in benediction or in diabolical mockery.

The scene *Prison* is of such tragic force that there is nothing in the eighteenth-century literature of Germany, or perhaps of any country, to compare with it. As far as Gretchen is concerned the power of this effect is partly due to the sheer pathos of the depiction of her wandering mind, reminiscent of the distraction of Ophelia, but even more to the pitiful distortion of the character we have known so intimately in previous scenes: the madly deformed yet recognisable versions of her physical passion for Faust (*4484–92*), of her love and respect for her mother (*4524, 4568–9*), of her timorousness (*4430, 4548*), her orderliness (*4521*ff.), her love of little children (*4552*). A particular poignancy attaches to the reflections, in this state of wretchedness, of earlier moments of happiness − 'they were happy times' (*4573*). In the course of the scene, more or less all that we have been shown of the relationship of Faust and Gretchen is briefly and touchingly recapitulated: the street in which they first met (*4475*), their conversation in Martha's garden (*4477*), Faust's words to her (*4488*) and the sound of his voice (*4461*), and the death of her brother (*4512–17*). Gretchen also tells of the things we know must have happened, though we have not seen them: their night of love (*4490, 4572–3*), the death of her mother (*4507, 4571*), the birth of her child (*4443–4*), its death at her hands (*4508, 4551–62*), her arrest and trial and loss of reputation (*4445–8*). She even looks forward in minute detail to the moment of her execution (*4587–95*). An entire narrative, the love affair from beginning to terrible end, is resumed within the compass of a single scene, which thereby lends an air of grim finality to a moment which might otherwise seem simply touching or nostalgic.

But the tragedy of the scene is also the tragedy of Faust. It is, after all, his doing that the day which should have been Gretchen's wedding-day, the day that should have ended her story (*4449*) with a 'lived happily ever after', is in fact to be the day of her execution (*4581*). It is as much his doing as Gretchen's that his child is now dead − and it is emphasised that the child was 'a gift' to both of them (*4509–10* cp. *3217*). This is the price he has paid for the life and freedom conferred by his wager with Mephistopheles. A series of futile laments culminates in a plea which shows up precisely the emptiness of the wager's reduction of life to an endless rush from moment to moment:

> Lass das Vergangne vergangen sein,
> Du bringst mich um. (*4518–19*)

Let bygones be bygones, you are killing me.

Even his increasingly frantic appeals to Gretchen to escape with him are vitiated by his original fateful choice, for in binding him to Mephistopheles, the spirit of negation, his wager put an ultimately insuperable barrier between him and her (*4534*). Gretchen knows as well as Mephistopheles, and better than Faust, that the claims of justice and retribution cannot for ever be conjured away by the magic with which Faust proposes to save her (*4547* cp. *Dark Day, Countryside*, line 44). There is not in the end even anything particularly noble about the defeat of Faust's great revolt – the moral squalor of his last appearance is nearer to irony than to tragedy.

What does suffuse this last scene with a nobility that raises it into the tragic sphere is a force that originates outside Faust altogether. That force is Gretchen's love for him, and its nobility lies precisely in its generosity: Faust does not deserve it, and yet it overflows, unaffected by all he has done to wound it. Since the middle of *Walpurgis Night* an element has been stirring in the play which suggests that the power of Mephistopheles is not irresistible nor his victory ultimate. Not because of anything Faust has himself done, but in so far as his mind has turned to Gretchen, in so far as he has recognised the claims of their love, he has in the last scenes escaped Mephistopheles' influence. Now Gretchen's love for Faust becomes tragic as it renounces for ever its fulfilment with him and instead accepts death in obedience to a higher law and a greater love. Deep within that love, into which Gretchen's love is assumed, there lies enclosed a seed of hope, the promise of redemption – even for Faust.

Lines 4405–59 (P189–91, E167–9)

We first find ourselves with Faust outside the door of Gretchen's dungeon. Despite the unfamiliar feeling of compassion for the human lot, Faust seems in control of himself (*4405–11*). From within there emerges a song, such as we have come to associate with Gretchen, but this is not a song of love or desire but a dreadful demented folk-song of half-comprehensible crime (*4412–20*). We follow Faust in.

When Gretchen was a stranger to us, she was referred to in the stage directions by her full name, Margarete, and then, as she became the object of affection and pity, was called by her diminutive. Now she is given dignity in her suffering by a return to the full form. Her first words after her song show her, however, as a poor creature, crazed by the animal fear of death (*4423, 4433*). She is deep in illusion: though Faust is in her thoughts, she mistakes him for the executioner come before his time; she imagines herself with the dead child and cannot acknowledge that she has killed it; she misunderstands his action in falling to his knees, and sees and hears the nearness of Hell.

Lines 4460–535 (P191–4, E169–71)

For the only time in the play Faust, whose language since he came into the dungeon has been stilted and self-conscious, addresses Gretchen by her name (*4460*). Immediately she recognises him, the chains which he has unlocked fall from her − a symbolic moment which is however fully explained in realistic terms (before *4427*) − the shadows of delusion begin to recede and even something of her old sensuality is recovered, though after the naive, uninhibited fashion of the witless (*4479–97*). Gretchen does not, however, yet understand why Faust is here or what kind of freedom he is offering her, and the delirium of delight at his return causes the picture of a false hope and a false redemption to form in her mind (*4463, 4473–4*). But the rescue she envisages is simply a resumption and repetition of the happy moments in their past, a flight into the irrecoverable (*4475–8*). Faust cannot and will not be drawn into a reliving of past moments: that would contradict the essence of his being after the wager. The only rescue he can offer her is to share his life, on the terms on which he lives it, and for that Gretchen is no more ready than she ever was: their worlds are still in collision. She feels that he is rejecting her in the very moment of coming to save her (*4493–4, 4453–4*). And we know in our own hearts that it would be no redemption of Gretchen's tragedy were it resolved into a happy ending that imprisoned her in an endless repetition of past joy. Not that that makes it any less agonising to watch her mind wandering away from its flashes of lucidity and childish affection into the memory of terrible crimes, which she no longer attempts to disclaim (*4507–17*), or else into the only concern the future holds for her, the arrangement of the family graves (*4520–9*), which the recollection of past love interrupts with fierce poignancy (*4530–1*).

Lines 4536–96 (P194–6, E171–4)

Gretchen at last realises, after a pitifully clouded fashion (*4542*), that Faust is offering her physical release from the prison. She only has to will her escape, he tells her; one step and she is free (*4543, 4564*). But Gretchen cannot will that step – 'I may not' she says (*Ich darf nicht, 4544*). If she were to join Faust in his aimless, unattached, magical wandering through the world, her conscience and the authorities she acknowledges would soon catch up with her (*4547, 4549*). Faust's promise to protect her (*4550*) occasions only a terrible crescendo of visions of what, to be effective, Faust's magic would have to undo. When the visions have reached their mute climax (*4595*) we know that Gretchen has instead embraced her constricted life, even though the sword pierces her heart also (*3590*), and has rejected Faust's path of un-nature and unreality. The renunciation which, in *Forest, Cavern*, Faust rejected, so poisoning his life and hers, she has achieved, and she has attained the self-possession which seemed to be Faust's at the beginning of the scene but which he has now lost. First she recalls, clearly at last, the most terrible event in her life: the moment when she drowned her child (*4551–62*), a moment dominated in her memory by the panic-stricken desire for rescue. To give the child life again, *that* would be rescue, redemption (*4562*), but can Faust offer that? A second nightmare vision of her dead mother associates the shadow of indelible guilt with the joy of her love for Faust (*4565–73*). Faust can now succeed in his mission only by violence (*4576*) – indeed his offer of magical release is itself an act of violence, that would, if successful, negate all that their love has meant (*4578*). He tries to impress on Gretchen that night is wearing into dawn (*4579* cp. *4506, 4429*), but provokes in her only the fantasy of a dawn parting, after a night of love, on the morning of her wedding-day (*4580–2*). But fantasy is fading with the night, and after promising herself a meeting later in the happy day (*4585*), Gretchen realises that there are not going to be any wedding festivities after all (*4586*), not even any compromised by her loss of reputation (*4583–4*). And now with mercilessly prophetic clarity she envisages the only event the day does hold in store for her, as far as the very moment when the executioner's sword is swung, the last moment of her conscious life. Presence at her public death, a sympathetic sharing in it (*4593–4*), is the only reunion Gretchen can promise Faust for today. If her words 'we shall see each other again' bear another meaning, a meaning for eternity, it is one of which Gretchen herself is unaware. For Gretchen drinks her bitter cup to the lees. As if unaided by any transcending faith or hope, as if dying on behalf of her beloved the post-Christian death of a modern Faust, she makes present to herself and to us a world drained of all meaning and all feeling by the imminent prospect of death:

>   Stumm liegt die Welt wie das Grab!   (*4595*)
>   (Mute lies the world, like the grave!)

The terrible flatness of this vision, the absolute prosaic finality of the line, is emphasised by the simple device of leaving it without a rhyme: the friendly concatenation of madrigal verses has come to a stop. Any redemptive power contained in Gretchen's renunciation of a magical life with Faust, in her knowing acceptance of this most real death, has been achieved despite the profoundest desolation it is in Goethe's power to imagine. In the face of it Faust can only acknowledge his entire life to have been in error (*4596*).

In a sense the story of Faust has now ended. His great venture lies in shipwreck, he himself is reduced to enfeebled despair. In this disaster it does not matter whether his wager, the means for living a consciously modern life without renunciation, has been won or lost. Yet Gretchen's love for him is unaltered, even though she is dying without him: the good he never dreamt of, the value, not that he makes, but that another *gives* to him, is now alone for us the meaning of his life. That meaning is there precisely because Gretchen has refused to share the life that Faust lives in virtue of his curse on the world, and in virtue of his denial, in the wager, of the world's intrinsic value. To share Faust's magical life she would have to share the premiss on which it is based, a premiss explicitly (*1604*) destructive of her love for him. In renouncing life with Faust, which by now means renouncing life altogether, she affirms her love, its value, and the value of Faust.

The dramatic embodiment of the destructive premiss of Faust's life is his compact with Mephistopheles, who 'cannot love a soul', and in the last lines of the play Goethe gives, through the intervention of Mephistopheles, a dramatic embodiment of the renunciation and redemption which is implicit in the final relationship between Faust and Gretchen, but is expressed by neither.

Lines 4597–612 (P196–7, E174)

The sudden entry of Mephistopheles completes the parallel between the two scenes, *A Summerhouse* and *Prison*, the only scenes in which all three principal characters are together at once, respectively the climax and the catastrophe in Faust' experience of love, and of life, under the sign of the wager

But the hint of discord, which concluded *A Summerhouse*, is here made explicit and then finally resolved. Gretchen recognises her enemy (*4602*) and his destructive intentions (*4604*), and that her death is now a sacred act, an affirmation of the holiness he has always sought to profane (*4603*). All Faust's pleas are resumed in a phrase which unambiguously asserts his intention to do violence to her will ('You *shall* live', *4604*), forcing Gretchen to come with him, and so with Mephistopheles, and Gretchen's response is equally unambiguous. She hands herself over, body and soul, to the divine tribunal (*4605*). Of that the representatives to her are her earthly judges, and she thus in this moment chooses death at their hands rather than life with Faust. In the anguish of separation she cries out that Faust, who even now chooses life with the Devil rather than death with Gretchen (*4606*), fills her with the same horror that she feels for his evil companion (*4610*). Rescue can now come only from God (*4607*).

In terms of dramatic action, the fates of Faust and Gretchen are by line *4610*, already divided, the crisis of their lives is already decided. Faust has finally turned his back on the 'constricted life', and Gretchen has sought refuge in her God, from whom alone she hopes for the love that may redeem her and, through her, Faust. But Goethe in his last two lines gives poetic expression and confirmation of the hope that lies unspoken in these decisions. At least since the *Walpurgis Night's Dream* a strand of literary self-consciousness has reappeared, last seen in *Study I* or *Witch's Kitchen*. Goethe's own appearance in the *Dream*, the quasi-operatic transition from that scene to *Dark Day, Countryside*, the manifestly poetic rather than dramatic appeal of the unstageable scene *Night, Open Country*, the poetic – or, in modern terms, cinematic – way in which we follow Faust's perceptions from outside the door into the interior of the dungeon, the significant use of the name-form 'Margarete', unrepresentable on the stage, the recurrent allusions to Ophelia – in all these peculiarities the poem *Faust* has been making its presence felt through and behind *Faust* the drama. Now Goethe concludes the whole play with a device that is essentially poetic and literary, rather than dramatic. He deliberately takes up and varies the puppet-play motif of the voice off-stage, announcing the judgement and damnation of Faust: he makes Mephistopheles, the Accuser, affirm Gretchen's guilt, and a Voice from Above assert her redemption (*4611*).

The purpose of this latter intervention is multiple. It permits the expression of the ultimate metaphysical confidence which the action has justified but which cannot properly be known or uttered (as in a drama of Schiller's it would, regardless of propriety, be uttered) by any of the characters. There is no evidence, indeed, that any of the characters hears the words of the Voice from Above – those words are directed not at the characters but at the audience. The last words of Mephistopheles and Gretchen (*4611–12*) simply recapitulate in a heightened form their old conflict for the soul of the now silent Faust: Mephistopheles brutally reasserts his authority, and Gretchen's thoughts and love remain with Faust, even though she has finally chosen her God and he has once again chosen the Devil. In this context the Voice from Above is not really a dramatic intervention, as which it would raise more questions than it answers, and would compromise the desolation which Gretchen's love transfigures. It is a literary allusion, the voice of the poet, masquerading as the voice of God, and reminding us that this poem is a special variation of a specific literary form: the puppet-play *Faust*. But it is a *Faust* in which the principal agent is a woman, and the principal theme is the possibility of redemption – and not only of Gretchen. If we reflect on this version of the Faust story, as this self-conscious allusion encourages us to do, we find that it contains one element which must restrain us from dismissing this Faust's life as pointless, or worse: this Faust was loved, and that love was more valuable to the woman who felt it than life with him than life itself. Even if such redemption cannot realistically be expressed in the words or actions of characters, it can be expressed in the poem that takes so much trouble, and itself shows so much love, in telling the story. This poem is, to be precise, a modern *Faust*, a *Faust* for a world which no longer has faith in voices from above but in which the love which that faith once protected, and which is now preserved pre-eminently in poetry, is more active for good than any other force.

Chapter 7

After *Part One*, and before

The redemptive conclusion of *Faust. Part One* is as final and complete in its way as the more desolate conclusion of *Urfaust*. But can it really be conclusive, the modern reader asks, like the readers of 1808, since this is said to be the end only of the first part of a larger work? *Faust. Part Two*, however, is not so much a sequel to *Part One* as a parallel – not another episode in the story, rather another picture in a diptych. A number of Goethe's works possess a similar binary structure, notably his two tragic novels, *The Sorrows of Young Werther* (1774) and *The Elective Affinities* (1809). In each of these, the fundamental conflict in the work is fully expounded and brought to what might be called a provisional catastrophe by the end of a first part, while a second part repeats and varies the themes and tragic conclusion of the first, on a higher plane and at a higher level of intensity. As, in Goethe's botanical theory, a flower repeats and varies the pattern of a leaf, so *Faust. Part Two* repeats and varies *Part One*, on the higher plane of the 'great world' of human history and culture, amid a vastly richer array of poetic effects. Faust's search for the substance of life on premises which preclude his experiencing it for more than a moment and which turn all to dust in his hands, his experience of Nature and his moral corruption, his end in vacuity and his redemption in a higher sense by the love of a mediator, these are as much the themes of *Part Two* as of *Part One*. Because the second part repeats, rather than follows, the first, no temporal or causal relation is ever explicitly established between them: *Part Two* begins simply with a healing sleep which cuts Faust off from the events of *Part One*, as if he were starting once more afresh. As at the end of Act Three of *Part Two*, in a similar hiatus, the magic cloak does its work of transporting Faust into 'new life'.

But *Faust* is more complex than the two-part novels, in that the episodes of the traditional story provide a superficially sequential structure spanning both Parts. The 'course' Mephistopheles promised Faust continues: he visits the Emperor's court, summons up Helen of Troy, begets with her a son, assists the Emperor in his wars, becomes a wealthy landowner and entrepreneur (a reminiscence perhaps of Weidmann's *Faust*), dies shortly after midnight, steeped in sin, and is claimed, though unsuccessfully, by the Devil. But beneath the appearance of progression through the established story, the true structure of *Part Two* is provided by repetitions, mirrorings, as the later Goethe calls them, of features of *Part One*. Faust's search for Helen, the revived embodiment of perfect classical beauty, reflects his pursuit of Gretchen, and the moment when he takes Helen's hand, in the very centre of the play, reflects the moment in *Part One* when he took the hand of Gretchen in the summerhouse: a high point in which the substance of life is not after all *grasped* by Faust but instead is *given* him from an external source, love in the case of *Part One*, beauty in *Part Two*. For a fleeting moment the régime of the wager is forgotten. Mephistopheles interrupts, in *Part Two* as in *Part One*, and in neither Part does the child born of this union live to maturity. In *Part Two* as in *Part One*, Faust drifts away from the influence of the woman who inspired him and enters a world both of deep evil and insubstantial illusion and deceit: in *Part One* the Walpurgis Night, in *Part Two* the world of politics and big business. Faust at last experiences, and shares in, the evil of the French Revolution and its consequences, from which he was deflected in *Walpurgis Night*: he expropriates and murders the last living representatives of the old régime, including a Wanderer, who may stand for Goethe himself.

Faust awakens, though much more bemusedly than in *Dark Day, Countryside*, to a realisation that he has rendered his life valueless by the very means he adopted to fill it with experience. He regrets his curse and endeavours to renounce the magic that entered his body in *Witch's Kitchen*. But as before it is far too late to undo the influence of negativity in his life or even to reduce his dependence on it: Mephistopheles continues to act as his agent even though unrecognised by Faust, who is blind and moribund after disowning the witch's rejuvenating potion. Just as he insisted on trying to rescue Gretchen by magical means, so now Faust summons up all his powers of self-delusion to transfigure the natural necessity of his death. Deprived now of the magic by which in the past he realised them, he returns to the inspiring but insubstantial visions which filled his mind before his agreement with Mephistopheles. He repeats the repudiation of worldly cares which preceded his original suicide gesture (*640–51*), but in all the long intervening years Faust has discovered no alternative to self-annihilation. By pronouncing, in the very moment in which he is dying anyway, the words forbidden by the wager on pain of death, he resists Nature to the last and transforms his dying into a deliberate act. As in *Part One*, then, Faust in *Part Two*, though he may be remorseful, is fundamentally unrepentant to the end: he dies as he lived. Any redemption cannot derive from what he has done, cannot in any sense be his deserts. If Faust is to be saved it cannot be *because* of his delusion and hardness of heart; it must be *in spite* of them. That, after all, is what redemption means. In *Part Two*, as in *Part One*, redemption comes from the true substance of life, which Faust has never more than momentarily glimpsed: from love, in the person of Gretchen, and from beauty, in the guise of poetry.

Faust's life ends as it began, in darkness. Mephistopheles passes what might seem the most realistic judgement on this or, in a post-Christian era, on any human life: that eternal unchanging nothingness would have been preferable to this pretence of being (*11595–603*). Would that he had never been born (*4596*). But what of the poem in which this pointless, and worse than pointless, nonentity has been chronicled? What of the wealth of understanding and delight that the telling of the story has given us? Is that also worthless? Beyond the margins of Faust's natural life on earth, and so beyond the reach of realistic literature, as of realistic judgements, a change of mode begins in *Faust*, the poem. It is no longer a poem in which Faust does or can speak: it becomes a poem in which he is spoken about. We enter a self-conscious framework of predominantly lyrical reflection on the drama that has passed before our eyes. What follows is not a further episode in that drama but a dramatisation of forces and tensions already present in Faust's state at the end of *Part One*, and in a higher, more intense form, at the end of his passage through *Part Two*.

Literary self-consciousness makes itself felt as a brutally ironic satyr-play in the first framework scene, *Deposition*, which shows that the vocabulary of bonds, devils, angels and the entire supernatural world of Christian tradition is not, in this reflective framework, to be taken at its face value – indeed, that one reason why Faust's story is not devastatingly tragic is that it is, all along, partly comic. The 'jokes' in *Faust*, however, as Goethe once remarked, are 'very serious'. But the seriousness of the last scene of all, *Mountain Chasms*, does not consist in the addition to Faust's story of certain religious assertions, not even of the assertion that, though Faust's permanent willingness for action is a necessary condition of his salvation, it is not sufficient unless he has also received the free gift of love (*11936–41*). The apparatus of Dante's heaven is all there, with Gretchen and a Doctor Marianus in the roles of Beatrice and St Bernard. The Virgin Mary, once the Mater Dolorosa, now the Mater Gloriosa, is present as the transcendent image of Gretchen, who herself welcomes 'Faust's immortal parts' with a transfigured version of her prayer of agony in *Town Wall, Alley*, and intercedes successfully on his behalf. The two female figures fuse into an 'eternally feminine' principle that draws 'us' on into the infinite (*12110–11*), and that 'us' is all-inclusive: it embraces angels, Faust, possibly even Mephistopheles, certainly us readers, and Goethe too. But the truly (*11803–4*) serious is 'indescribable' (*12108*), and was as adequately, or inadequately, intimated by the irony of *Deposition* as now by mystical symbol. Of that indescribable goodness of life to us, the principal evidence that Goethe's poem furnishes is its own existence, its being given to us, and the principal symbol of that goodness, within the poem, is Gretchen's gift of love to Faust.

The last scenes of *Part Two* are the expansion, the flowering, of what lies so to speak in bud at the end of *Part One*, in the words of the Voice from Above and the last utterances of Mephistopheles and Gretchen. But they also complete a framework to Faust's story which began in three preliminary sections located before the beginning of *Part One*. These preliminary sections, however, are not only the first element in a framework which encloses the whole of *Faust. A Tragedy*; they are also, when taken together with the closing lines of *Part One*, a framework to *Part One* itself. And because the entire cycle of Faust's course, from darkness to darkness, is already run by the end of *Part One*, there is a perfectly good justification for the traditional practice of reading and performing these sections together with *Part One*, even if *Part Two* does not follow. Because to fail to distinguish clearly between the picture and its frame can lead to a serious misplacing of emphasis, we have here looked first at the picture. But provided the distinction is not forgotten, we may if we wish read the preliminary material as a preparation for *Part One* alone.

All three of the prolegomena share the essential characteristic of the framework scenes: that in them Faust does not and cannot speak, and their titles mark them off from the body of the play even more distinctly than *Deposition* and *Mountain Chasms*. Yet they are more continuous with one another than appears at first sight and they ease our passage into the play, much as the last scenes expand the play so that it incorporates us, its readers, of whatever time or place. The self-consciousness with which we begin, in the opening poem *Dedication* (*1–32*; P29–30, Exix), is absolutely specific, however: Goethe in the late 1790s musing on the resumption of work on a poem from which he last gave readings, and on which he was last continuously engaged, over twenty years before, and which contains pictures of his own 'first love and friendship' (*12*). The theme has become strange to him; his stern classical taste, secure in its possession of the firm shapes of ancient art (*30–1*), is unsettled by the desires and illusions of this shifting world of spirits. He himself has changed since 1775 and so has the world around him. His potential audience has changed too: no longer a gathering of a few friends in the intimacy of a semi-dramatic reading, it is the unknown mass of the reading public, in which the occasional kindred soul is now probably unreachable (*21–4*).

By the end of *Dedication* it is already established that the 'realities' (*32*) that are to follow are something that has 'disappeared'; they are memories, the contents of a reflective consciousness. In the *Prelude on the Stage* (*33–242*; P31–7, E1–7) we take a first step into that consciousness; the Goethe of autobiography and the 'poetry of experience' (*Erleb-nislyrik*) is lost to view, and we find ourselves in a dramatic discussion between a Theatre Manager, a Poet, and a Clown, about the social function of the work of art which, in one sense, is still to follow but which, in another sense, has already begun. This last ambiguity is reflected in the reader's gradual progress into an ever more fictitious world as the scene wears on: the audience which at the start is already assembled to watch the play and is indirectly addressed (*39–42*) is gradually forgotten, and the play which at the start of the *Prelude* is still unwritten begins immediately the scene is over, as we are plunged, presumably, into the imagination of the Poet. Continuity and discontinuity with *Dedication* are both clearly established: the theme of public reception is common to the poem and to the *Prelude*, but in the *Prelude* the public discussed is no longer the reading public for *Faust* the book, but a fictitious theatrical audience which is being enter-tained by travelling troupes of a period no later than the 1760s, not by the established commercial repertory companies of the 1790s. The Poet speaks at first in the same stanzaic form that Goethe used in *Dedication* (*59–74*), but, as himself a character on the stage, he is not identifiable with the author of that poem, and this anyway becomes apparent from the opinions he utters.

The three-cornered discussion, taken as a whole, is however a movingly complex expression of Goethe's attitude to his art as he approached the age of fifty. Even the Manager, who has a sharp eye for the realities of literary life (*102–3, 115–16*), is not a man of straw, although he voices the commercial considerations of the impresario. The Poet by contrast has a high vision of poetry's purpose, evidently much influenced by Schiller, for he sees in Nature only the endless monotony of a single unchanging principle, which the artist turns into rhythm, harmony and meaning (*142–7*). The Clown modifies this aristocratic, Idealist conception, by pointing out that the variety thus required of the poet's production can be achieved only by a more realistic art that accepts the dangers of imperfection and fragmentariness (*158–83*). The Poet does not disagree, but complains that this art was something he, like the author of *Dedication*, could practise when youth and love inspired it, but youth and love are now lost and with them its very foundation (*184–97*). The Clown begs to differ: there is an art that conceals art, a supremely controlled apparent improvisation that is best practised by the middle-aged who are not afraid to acknowledge the child within them (*206–13*). All this, no doubt, is the manner of the play that is to come: the wealth and brilliance of effect demanded by the Manager, the apparent artlessness and realistic allusiveness which for the Clown constitute maturity, and the passionate celebration of the capacity of art to give meaning to the emptiness of natural existence which justifies the Poet's vocation and is fired ultimately by his powers of love. The curtains on the little stage are drawn back, and we step through into the work we have just heard discussed.

And still we do not touch 'realities' – only a Prologue to them. If we are reminded of the fictitious nature of the *Prelude* by the preceding *Dedication*, the *Prelude* itself performs the same function (*242*) for the *Prologue in Heaven* (*243–353*; P39–42, E9–12) (written, like the rest of the prefatory material, in the period 1797–1800). In conception and execution the *Prologue* is intended to resemble a mummers' or mystery play performed with exiguous theatrical resources, as the laconic stage directions suggest, and no other scene in the entire work makes consistent use of this particular fiction until we come to *Deposition* at the end of *Part Two*. The religious apparatus of the scene should not be taken significantly more seriously than that of *Deposition* or *Mountain Chasms*, as the comical tone anyway indicates (*296, 350–3*). In *Dedication* we reflected on *Faust*, the poem, as a product of Goethe's life; in the *Prelude* we reflected on *Faust*, the play, as a work of art; in the *Prologue* we now reflect on the story of Faust, the man – who is here named for the first time – as a metaphysical or moral parable. We consider, not its form, but its meaning. Considering the meaning of a story is not the same thing as telling a story, and we should beware of the temptation to read the *Prologue* as if it were the first episode in Faust's story, the first scene of *Part One*. It is still a part of the meditative framework. Confusion may arise because, as with the two preceding sections, its relation to the 'realities' that follow it changes as it progresses. Although *Dedication* and the *Prelude* are linked to each other by the figure of the Poet, there is no such link between the *Prelude* and the *Prologue*. Instead, the *Prologue* shares one character – but only one – with the main drama: Mephistopheles. (The Voice from Above, at the end of *Part One*, belongs, strictly speaking to the framework. It is left uncertain whether we hear the voice of the Lord, or the voice of the Poet.) In this respect also the *Prologue* corresponds to the penultimate framework scene *Deposition*, which is principally devoted to a transition from Mephistopheles to the world of the heavenly hosts. Indeed, the purpose of the *Prologue* turns out, by the time it is over, to have been far more to tell us about Mephistopheles than to tell us about the Lord and the order of His universe.

The majestic opening strophes chanted by the archangels (*243–70*), and dealing in order with the solar system, the earth, and the natural forces operating on the earth, certainly suggest that combination in divinity of harmony and power, light and darkness, positive and negative, which will later be alluded to by the Lord himself. But the grandeur of the archangels' theme contrasts ironically with the limitations of their stage presence, and by comparison with the intruding cynic or jester Mephistopheles they seem like self-important or supercilious courtiers (275, 279, 282 cp. 290). Mephistopheles quickly reduces the scale of the discussion to that of the human world, where a divine order does not seem very apparent. It might therefore seem, as the overt parallels with the opening of the Book of Job (1:6–12) also suggest, that we are here to be concerned mainly with one of the eighteenth century's favourite problems, theodicy, the justification of the ways of God to men. But our scope is narrowed still further: to the case of Faust, and his own peculiar, far from typical behaviour (300). The principal question, therefore, posed by the Prologue is only indirectly a question of theodicy. It is the question whether Faust's soul will be saved, or whether the confusions and wrongdoings in which all human beings are involved during their mortal active lives (317, 328–9) will so blind and corrupt him that the spark of divinity (284) in him will ultimately be extinguished and he will have been finally detached from his divine origin (312, 324). Now this is not at all the question that Faust asks about his life, when he makes his wager in Study II. It is, much more nearly, the question that we the readers ask about the outcome of his compact with Mephistopheles – whether the events that follow will prove Faust right or the Devil (see above on lines 1712–1867). The answer here hinted at is the answer which the play in fact provides: that the Devil may have a better understanding of Faust and of the pragmatic consequences of his actions than Faust does himself, but even the Devil's understanding is not the last word there is to be said about him (325 cp. 1676–7). We are not however being offered in the Prologue any anticipation of the internal course of the drama. The one point in the Prologue relevant to our understanding of the action of Part One is something anyway given in the traditional characterisation of Mephistopheles: his hidden, metaphysical, intention in entering on his relationship with Faust. We are told what the wager will hold for him: the possibility of tempting Faust into damnation.

The question posed by the dialogue between the Lord and Mephistopheles is not, however, completely identical with the question left in our minds, as readers, by *Study II*. The issue in *Study II* is between the Devil and a post-Christian man whose intended way of life presupposes the non-existence both of the Lord and of the Lord's perspective on things. The profoundest tension in the play is thus one that *cannot* be established in a prologue in Heaven. Of that tension and its possible resolution, Goethe's *Prologue* provides what is, necessarily, only a metaphor, and the distinction between the real tension in the play and its metaphorical expression and resolution in the *Prologue* and *Mountain Chasms* is the distinction between the picture and its framework.

Despite what is often said, no wager is concluded in Heaven between Mephistopheles and the Lord. (Just as, on earth, Mephistopheles shows little interest in the wager that is of such importance for Faust). The Lord is above such things and does not respond to Mephistopheles' offer of a bet (*312*). He merely gives Mephistopheles permission to continue being the Devil he is and asserts that even such negativity will be outwitted in the end and made to serve the good purposes of His creation (*316, 323, 343*). In so far as it is Mephistopheles who leads Faust to Gretchen and Helen, to the powers that ultimately will secure his redemption, the Lord will be proved right. But even that redemption is a matter of the play's metaphysical and interpretative framework, not of its dramatic core − it never crosses Faust's mind to ask whether he is, or can be, redeemed. The Lord's bland and jovial unflappability reflects a vital fact about the *Prologue* − that, like the Lord, it is dramatically superfluous. The central tension in the play is not supplanted in our minds by any question of theodicy, by any agreement about Faust's 'immortal parts' made between Mephistopheles and a Lord who never appears again. It remains the tension established in *Study II* and maintained throughout the Gretchen story, between the post-Christian life of Faust and the 'constricted life' of renunciation hitherto associated with Christianity. The 'meaning' which the *Prologue* invites us to find in the tragic outcome to this tension is a transcendent redemption by love, which is presented as a Christian mystery more profound, because closer to the nature of poetry, than any talk of damnation, Hell, or indeed Heaven — all of which are only ever treated ironically. The Lord associates Himself, in His concluding lines, with the power of love (*347*), which makes available to the Archangels — and also to us readers — what is concealed from Mephistopheles and, for all but two moments of his life, from Faust: the wealth of living beauty (*345*) in a world of limited (*347*) and therefore changing creatures (*346*), in which none the less intellect can discern eternal form and value (*348–9*). Even if only in a humorous intimation of the inexpressible, Goethe thus hints at a poetic vision of a universal harmony transcending even the ferocious contradictions which will be embodied for Faust in the Spirit of Earth. The love which began as Goethe's private experience in *Dedication*, and grew into the Poet's inspiring passion in *Prelude*, has now become a great river, sustaining the sun and its 'fellow spheres' and which at the end of *Mountain Chasms* will sweep us all away.

But, even if we choose not to employ the terminology of 'damnation', we may still be allowed to doubt the omnipotence of a love of which the only ultimately secure refuge is the poem itself, and of which the only negation ultimately admitted is apathy, the nihilist despair voiced by Mephistopheles on Faust's death, and by Faust himself in Gretchen's dungeon. For when Faust is brought face to face with that, Goethean, divine love — the love which the poem shows towards its subject-matter — he is, precisely *redeemed* (and the same is probably true of Mephistopheles in *Deposition*). It remains uncertain whether either Goethe's Lord, or much of the eighteenth-century theology which he represents — or perhaps, to be fair, our own age, intellectually so deeply indebted to the age of Goethe — has the strength to acknowledge that the confrontation with love may also be a *judgement*. Confrontation in *Faust*, essentially a monodrama enclosed within the musings of a poet, is anyway rare. Where it does occur, in *Part One*, in the collision of Gretchen's world and Faust's, and in the renunciation that follows, the play does perhaps show that − tragic − strength. Certainly in *Part Two*, however, both confrontation and judgement will be sought in vain: though irony can do much, it is not finally a substitute for them. Of the last 'framework' scene, *Mountain Chasms*, we may feel that he only has earned the right to share in the vision of love in Dante's Paradise who has seen that same love in the power that laid the foundation of Dante's Hell:

> Giustizia mosse il mio alto fattore;
> fecemi la divina potestate,
> la somma sapienza e il primo amore.

(Justice moved my sublime creator; I was made by divine power, by highest wisdom and by original love.)

To the first love of which these words speak, affixed as they are on the sombre gates, beyond which, by the choice of those who pass them, all hope dies, to a love which expresses itself in human freedom, and in the suffering incarnation of divine justice, there is no equivalent in Goethe's poem.

Chapter 8

Faust's posterity

It was Goethe's doing alone that Doctor Faust entered the nineteenth century as a supreme literary symbol, and not as the squeaking puppet to which the eighteenth century had reduced him. All the other attempts to press his story into the service of the German national literary revival had failed more or less signally, though an exception might be made of F. Klinger's bitter novel of 1791, *Faust's Life, Deeds and Damnation*, in which Faust is identified with the inventor of printing. After the publication of *Faust. A Fragment* in 1790, and of *Part One* in 1808, the history of the Faust myth is the history of reactions to Goethe, in imitation or rejection. The libretto, by J. K. Bernard, of Spohr's opera, *Faust* (1816), though nominally independent, and ending with Faust's damnation, is influenced by Goethe at several essential points. Already in Goethe's lifetime numerous imitations of his work appeared, including, incredibly, attempts to provide the still missing *Part Two*, and the work of critical exposition and interpretation began, notably with K. E. Schubarth's two-volume study *In Appraisal of Goethe* (1818, 1820). The appeal of Goethe's play to the burgeoning Romantic movement of Europe was immediate and powerful. In 1804 Adalbert von Chamisso published a dramatic poem, *Faust*, which takes up, though in a tragic sense, the Idealist philosophical themes of the *Fragment*, and in his world-famous story of *Peter Schlemihl* (1814), who sells his shadow to the Devil and so makes himself an outcast from human society, there are clear Faustian overtones. The Romantic conception of Faust appears most vividly in the visual arts, in the Nazarene Peter Cornelius' *Faust-Cycle* (1811–16) and in Delacroix' illustrations to *Part One* (1827), to both of which Goethe gave a cool but not unfriendly welcome. Faust as the accursed and wandering outsider recurs in C. D. Grabbe's *Don Juan and Faust* (1829), strongly influenced Byron's *Manfred* (1817), and *The Deformed Transformed* (1824), as Byron himself acknowledged, and may have contributed some motifs to James Hogg's *Confessions of a Justified Sinner* (1824). The first reasonably full translation of *Part One* into English was Lord Frances Gower's of 1823, but Goethe was distressed by its inadequacies. Coleridge, however − whom Shelley thought ideal for the task − decided against translating *Faust*, objecting to its obscenity and blasphemy. It was not until after Goethe's death that the play, along with the rest of German literature, emerged in England from its reputation for atheism and Jacobinism, becoming known and admired, if from a distance, in a series of Victorian and twentieth-century versions.

After Goethe's death, and the publication of *Part Two*, in 1832, European reactions to Goethe's work take a negative turn, largely perhaps because of scepticism about his Faust's later career and redemption. Nikolaus Lenau's semi-dramatic poem *Faust* (1836) is nihilistically tragic while Heine's ballet scenario *Doctor Faust* (1851) explicitly counters the untraditional abstractions of *Part Two*. Berlioz' 'dramatic legend', *The Damnation of Faust* (1846), witnesses to a general feeling that Goethe had successfully modernised the Faust story by introducing into it the Gretchen theme, but would have done better to leave the traditional ending untouched. Gounod's opera *Faust* (1859) concentrates on the love story but manages to retain something of the ambiguity of the conclusion of *Part One*, while Boito's attempt to introduce elements of *Part Two* and Faust's redemption (*Mephistopheles*, 1868, revised 1875) met at first with little approval.

In the reactions to Goethe's masterpiece both of poets and other artists, and of literary critics, in the middle and later nineteenth century, it is possible to see certain misconceptions about the work which have decisively influenced interpretation of it down to the present day. Chief among these must be the failure to recognise the critical, even dialectical, relation of the poem to the currents of thought and moral attitudes of its own time. Once the more obvious satirical elements, such as the *Walpurgis Night's Dream* or several scenes in *Part Two*, are held to be extraneous to the action, it becomes more easily possible to overlook the exceptional and unnatural character of Faust's ambitions, even of his agreement with the Devil, and to transform him from an example of forces which Goethe thought specifically modern and highly destructive into a representative of all humanity – even of all the best in humanity. This misconception is compounded if the delicately complex structure of the completed work is not appreciated. The balance Goethe establishes between the darkness and emptiness of Faust's death in the drama, properly so called, and the redemption in the meditative framework, is ignored and it is assumed that at the end of *Part Two* Goethe's Faust is simply saved. *Part Two* is held to be a straightforward continuation of *Part One*, and the Gretchen story, instead of being as nearly final a judgement on Faust's career as any that is passed in the work, is seen as but an episode, even a necessary stepping-stone, in Faust's progress. Gretchen's intercession for Faust in the meditative framework now seems too incidental a factor to account for his redemption, and the cause for it is sought not outside Faust – where alone it can be found – but somewhere in the works of his life, in a supposed 'development' or 'purification', or even in his final, peculiarly devilish, involvement in the world of politics and social engineering.

These misconceptions remained relatively undeveloped for as long as *Part Two* was not taken seriously and the more obviously tragic *Part One* was held to be the fullest expression of Goethe's genius – as by F. T. Vischer in his exhilarating parody *Faust. A Tragedy. Part the Third* (1862). But after the establishment of Bismarck's Empire in the period 1866–72, when it became necessary to invent a pantheon of German literary classics to adorn the new nation's claim to parity with other European powers, the stock of *Part Two* gradually rose and not only among nationalists, as is evidenced by the sublime setting of *Mountain Chasms* in Mahler's Eighth

Symphony (1907). Thus there emerged a peculiarly and pro-
grammatically German Faust – one Second Empire critic
actually saw in the maritime activities at the end of *Part Two*
a prophecy of the German Navy League – a Faust who,
driven by the tragic necessity of his 'striving', 'had to' shatter
the limited, Catholic and therefore un-German world of Gretchen in order to scale the heights of pagan classical culture,
and to turn at last to useful work on behalf of the people
('Volk'). Although this regrettably involved murders, these
were tragically, or historically, necessary and Faust had none
the less, or therefore, deserved redemption. This grotesque
travesty of Goethe's subtle poem was sanctified by the invention of the term 'Faustian' (*das Faustische*) to describe
modern humanity since the Renaissance, striving upward,
especially in Germany, and through the toils of necessary
guilt, towards some indeterminate collective goal, or possibly
no goal at all. The nationalist interpretation of Faust
culminated in O. Spengler's application of his name to a
whole category of human history (*The Decline of The West*,
1918–22). By this course, alas, even *Faust* became a tributary
to the ideology of National Socialism. However, Marxist
interpretations, particularly those of G. Lukács (*Faust
Studies*, 1940, published in *Goethe und seine Zeit*, Bern,
1947; English translation by Robert Anchor, *Goethe and his
Age*, London, 1968), use much the same conceptual
apparatus and make much the same assumptions about the
structure and intentions of the text. Despite the efforts of
several enlightened critics after the First, and particularly after
the Second, World War, a modified version of the Second
Empire *Faust* is the received wisdom in both Germanies today.

The outstanding twentieth-century versions of the Faust
story have naturally tried to avoid the Bismarckian shadow
cast by what was held to be Goethe's version, but in so doing
they have returned closer than most modern critics to
Goethe's original spirit. Busoni's opera *Doctor Faust* (1922)
draws on the puppet-play to produce a sinister tragedy sur-
prisingly close in atmosphere to *Urfaust*. Thomas Mann's
novel *Doctor Faustus* (1947), which puts its story in parallel

with Germany's decline into National Socialism, draws principally on the Faust Book of 1587. But Mann has rediscovered the possibility of that dialectical use of the legend in criticism of the contemporary age which, in a less grim and hectic form, was a distinguishing if neglected feature of both Parts of Goethe's work. Goethe's wager scene can certainly bear comparison with the self-consciously modernist theological and philosophical argument of Paul Valéry's *My Faust* (1946), and partly anticipates its reversal of the traditional relationship between Faust and the Devil. Modern poets writing in English have shown some sympathy for the encyclopaedic aspects of Goethe's poem, particularly *Part Two* (see Peter Redgrove, *Doctor Faust's Sea-Spiral Spirit*, London, 1972; Thomas Kinsella, '*hesitate, cease to exist, glitter again*', in *New Poems 1973*, Dublin, 1973). Traces of a nostalgic respect for Gretchen and her values remain in D. J. Enright's witty, erudite and parodistic meditations on the entire Faust tradition, and particularly on Goethe's play (*A Faust Book*, Oxford, 1979). Otherwise, the story of Faust and Gretchen, which so moved our Romantic and Victorian forebears, and which has claims to be Goethe's greatest tragic achievement, has found little echo in recent literature.

Guide to further reading

Despite its antiquity and despite its avowed preference for Goethe's earlier period, the classic biography of Goethe in English is still G. H. Lewes's *The Life and Works of Goethe* (London, 1855). R. Friedenthal's rather sensational biography was published in English translation as *Goethe, His Life And Times*, in 1965 (London). An excellent brief modern survey, more even-handed than Lewes's, is T. J. Reed, *Goethe* (Oxford, 1984), and Barker Fairley's *A Study of Goethe* (Oxford, 1947) is an indispensable literary treatment of the period up to 1786. F. J. Lamport, *A Student's Guide to Goethe* (London, 1971) does wonders in its small compass. For the reader of German the short illustrated biography by Peter Boerner (Reinbek, 1964) is useful and attractive. Goethe's *Conversations with Eckermann* (Everyman edition, translated by J. Oxenford, London, 1971) is an agreeable introduction to the older poet, but unreliably reports his views on Faust.

There are numerous standard studies of *Faust* written in English: of the more recent, S. Atkins *Goethe's Faust: a Literary Analysis* (Cambridge, Mass., 1958) covers the entire work, while E. C. Mason's *Goethe's Faust. Its Genesis and Purport* (Berkeley and Los Angeles, 1967) deals principally with *Part One*. W. H. Bruford's *Faust I, Scene by Scene* (London, 1968) published in parallel with his annotated edition of the text, is invaluable for the reader of German but now difficult of access. Bruford's notes to the Everyman edition, though few, are excellent. The liveliest account in any language of the various literary forms taken by the Faust story, from the original Faust book to Thomas Mann, is E. M. Butler, *The Fortunes of Faust* (Cambridge, 1952). Two essays in English of particular interest are Erich Heller,

'Goethe and the Avoidance of Tragedy', in his book *The Disinherited Mind* (Cambridge, 1952; 4th edn, London, 1975) and L. A. Willoughby, 'Goethe's Faust: A Morphological Approach', in E. M. Wilkinson and L. A. Willoughby, *Goethe: Poet and Thinker* (London, 1962). *Goethe's Faust Part One. Essays in Criticism*, edited by J. B. Vickery and J. Sellery (Belmont, Calif., 1969), collects a score of different views, and the Norton Critical Edition of the play includes a revealing cross-section of German opinions in English translation.

The German 'literature', as it is pleasantly called, relating to *Faust* is of course endless, though the five volumes of the *Faust–Bibliographie* edited by H. Henning (Berlin and Weimar, 1966–76) are comprehensive up until their terminal date. None the less some of the standard works of late-nineteenth-century so-called 'positivist' (i.e. factually based) scholarship have still not been replaced, e.g. O. Pniower, *Goethes Faust. Zeugnisse und Excurse zu seiner Entstehungsgeschichte* (Berlin, 1899), or J. Minor, *Goethes Faust. Entstehungsgeschichte und Erklärung*, 2 vols. (Stuttgart, 1901). The most useful modern guide to the whole of *Faust* is also one of the cheapest and most readily available, the Reclam *Kommentar zu Goethes Faust* by T. Friedrich and L. J. Scheithauer (Stuttgart, 1973), which has been kept reasonably up-to-date since its first publication in 1932, though the interpretative sections of the introduction should be treated with care. Only in 1982 did modern German scholarship produce a full-scale, line-by-line commentary on *Faust. Part One*: Hans Arens's *Kommentar zu Goethes Faust I* (Heidelberg, 1982) is extensive rather than exhaustive, but it does some justice to the literary wealth of its subject. An essential anthology of critical and scholarly studies, from Vischer to the present day, is provided by *Aufsätze zu Goethes 'Faust I'*, edited by Werner Keller (Wege der Forschung 145, Darmstadt, 1974); and Valters Nollendorfs, *Der Streit um den Urfaust* (The Hague, 1967), is a remarkable achievement of modern 'positivism'. A stimulating essay in German by Erich Heller is 'Warum der Darsteller des Faust es schwer hat, die

Paktszene richtig zu sprechen', in his *Essays über Goethe* (Frankfurt, 1970). Classics of the late-nineteenth- and early-twentieth-century approach to *Faust* include the two-volume edition by G. Witkowski (Leipzig, 1906), F. Gundolf, *Goethe* (Berlin, 1969), and K. Viëtor, *Goethe. Dichtung, Wissenschaft, Weltbild* (Bern, 1949). Important steps towards an understanding of the play liberated from the inheritance of the Second Reich have been: W. Krogmann, *Goethes 'Urfaust'* (Germanistische Studien 143, Berlin, 1933); K. Burdach, 'Das religiöse Problem in Goethes Faust', *Euphorion* 33 (1932) 3–26; W. Böhm, *Faust der Nichtfaustische* (Halle, 1933); H.-O. Burger, 'Motiv, Konzeption, Idee – das Kräftespiel in der Entwicklung von Goethes Faust', *Deutsche Vierteljahrsschrift* 20 (1942) 17–63; W. Flitner, *Goethe im Spätwerk* (Hamburg, 1947); E. Staiger, *Goethe* (3 vols., Zurich and Freiburg, 1952–9); and H. Schwerte, *Faust und das Faustische. Ein Kapitel deutscher Ideologie* (Stuttgart, 1962). The technicalities of scholarly speculation are seductive, however, and there has been a regrettable tendency in recent years to discuss the *Faust* or *Fausts* Goethe might have written but did not – hence perhaps the paucity of full-length commentaries. A word of warning is therefore necessary against the irrelevancies and mystifications of E. Grumach's 'Prolog und Epilog im Faustplan von 1797', *Goethe* 14/15 (1952/3) 92–104, which has proved unfortunately influential.

I have developed further some of the points touched on in this book in two essays: 'Approaching Faust I', *Journal of European Studies* 8 (1978), 175–202; and ' "Du ahnungsloser Engel du!" ': Some current views of Goethe's *Faust*', *German Life and Letters* N.S.36 (1982/3) 116–47.

The more important texts referred to in Chapter 1 are conveniently available as follows: the Faust Book of 1587 in *Deutsche Volksbücher*, ed. K. O. Conrady (Rowohlts Texte Deutscher Literatur, n.p., 1968); C. Marlowe, *Doctor Faustus*, ed. K. Walker (Edinburgh, 1973); G. E. Lessing, *D. Faust. Die Matrone von Ephesus. Fragmente*, ed. K. S. Guthke (Reclam 6719, Stuttgart, 1968).